# What's Next After Wicca?

## Non-Wiccan Occult Practices and Traditional Witchcraft

### Sophia diGregorio

# OTHER BOOKS BY SOPHIA DIGREGORIO

Practical Black Magic: How to Hex and Curse Your Enemies

Traditional Witches' Formulary and Potion-making Guide: Recipes for Magical Oils, Powders and Other Potions

How to Write Your Own Spells for Any Purpose and Make Them Work

Grimoire of Santa Muerte: Spells and Rituals of Most Holy Death, the Unofficial Saint of Mexico (Santa Muerte Series) (Volume 1)

Grimoire of Santa Muerte, Vol. 2: Altars, Meditations, Divination and Witchcraft Rituals for Devotees of Most Holy Death
(Santa Muerte Series) (Volume 2)

The Occult Files of Sophia diGregorio Bitcoin and Altcoins Patronage Program: How to Join Our Cryptocurrency-Based Patronage Program and Why We are Doing Things This Way

Traditional Witches' History of the Occult Banking System: How Witches and Occultists Can Use Bitcoin and Altcoins for Privacy and Anti-Discrimination by Sophia diGregorio

The Occult Files of Sophia diGregorio: The Public Monologues of 2018

# What's Next After Wicca?

Non-Wiccan Occult Practices and Traditional Witchcraft

by

Sophia diGregorio

2019

Winter Tempest Books

*What's Next After Wicca? Non-Wiccan Occult Practices and Traditional Witchcraft*

Copyright © 2019 Sophia diGregorio

All rights reserved.

ISBN: 1-949999-03-3
ISBN-13: 978-1-949999-03-7

This is the first paperback edition of this book. The ebook edition of it was originally published by Winter Tempest Books on April 12, 2012.

Cover Image: *The Three Witches from Shakespeare's Macbeth* by Daniel Gardner, 1775. PD-Shakko. https://commons.wikimedia.org

License statement: This document contains material protected under copyright laws. Any unauthorized reprint, transmission or resale of this material without the express permission of the author is strictly prohibited. No part of this book may be used or reproduced in any manner whatsoever without written permission from the author except in the case of brief quotations embodied in critical articles and reviews.

# DEDICATION

To my customers and friends from the store and all the friends I haven't met yet who are relentlessly searching for answers to life's most profound questions.

# CONTENTS

| | | |
|---|---|---|
| 1 | Introduction | 1 |
| 2 | What is Wicca? | 3 |
| 3 | How Do People Become Wiccans? | 9 |
| 4 | The Attraction of Wicca | 13 |
| 5 | Benefits of Wicca | 17 |
| 6 | Why Wicca is Rejected by Many Occultists | 19 |
| 7 | Non-Wiccan Religions, Organizations and Philosophies | 25 |
| 8 | Traditional Witchcraft | 37 |
| 9 | How to Become a Student of the Occult | 45 |
| 10 | On Coming Out of the Closet | 49 |
| 11 | What's Next After Wicca? | 53 |
| | References | 69 |

# CHAPTER 1
# INTRODUCTION

By some estimates, Wicca is one of the fastest growing religions in the world. Although, because of the independent and private nature of many practitioners, it is difficult to arrive at any good estimates of the number of Wiccans. Unquestionably, Wicca is the most accessible and acceptable form of witchcraft.

Wicca is important to any modern discussion of the occult because it is the means by which many people take their first step out of Christianity and the oppressive mindset that grips some aspects of our culture. This has been especially true in the past 20 years or more since the appearance of Wicca in popular culture, in particular movies and television.

It is a refuge for many people, especially those who have experienced spiritual abuse at the hands of patriarchal religion and culture. It is the final stop for many who are looking for spiritual answers. They embrace Wicca wholeheartedly and remain Wiccan for the rest of their lives.

But, for many more people it is only the beginning of a journey in which exploring Wicca is one small step on the path to enlightenment. It is for those people that this book is intended.

"What's Next After Wicca?" explores the attraction of Wicca and then goes on to look at other alternative beliefs and theories. It, also, looks at Satanism, Luciferianism, Gnosticism, traditional witchcraft and the roots of the New Age movement, which are all too often overlooked by newcomers.

This book grew out of a question the author often heard from customers at her metaphysical bookstore after they had explored all of the most popular books about Wicca for about one year. They would ask, "What else is there?"

The people who asked this question were frustrated with mainstream Wiccan books and publications that seem to be the same information rehashed and regurgitated by one author after another. Some of them, also, felt that identifying themselves as Wiccan was not allowing them to fully express their true nature.

The purpose of this book is to provide information along with more avenues of research for people who are looking for something more and who deeply desire complete intellectual freedom in the pursuit of answers about the nature of the world.

It is the author's intention to show both the benefits and limitations of Wicca and to show that there are many other fascinating aspects of the occult to explore.

# CHAPTER 2
# WHAT IS WICCA?

The term, "Wicca," is derived from an Old Saxon term for "witch." It was mostly forgotten until its use was resurrected in England in the 1950s by a witchcraft-based religion in the form of numerous covens, which would bear that name.

The most popular of these was begun by an English witch named Gerald Gardner. But there were other notable Wiccan covens with similar beliefs and structures being formed at the same time. Among these was what would later be known as the Coven of Atho, which was founded by an English Wiccan by the name of Charles Cardell. Another called Cochranianism or Cochrane's Craft was founded in 1951 by Robert Cochrane. In the 1960s, a very important offshoot of Gardnerian Wicca, which still enjoys some popularity, known as Alexandrian Wicca, was established by Alexander and Maxine Sanders.

With some variations, this neo-pagan, religious reconstruction shared certain commonalities in the worship of a Great Horned God and a triple goddess. The religion revolved around a year-long celebration of nature, with eight primary sabbats or high holy days. Rituals were typically conducted in the nude or "sky-clad" to remind members that they were free beings.

Wiccans, then and now, revere nature, which is seen as neither good nor evil. They do not believe in an evil force, a fact which they are in the position of frequently reiterating in the face of Christian accusations of devil worship.

The true history of Wicca is obscured, in part, because up until the year 1951, witchcraft and related practices, such as mediumship, were illegal in England. In that year, the last of England's succession of Witchcraft Acts, dating back to the middle of the 16th century, were finally repealed.

Afterward, witches, mediums and psychics in England were more able to live their lives without fear of running afoul of the law. Many of the early founders and members of Wicca claimed to have ancient witch lineage. But, prior to that time, they were forced to live in the shadows. This fact, together with the secrecy characteristic of covens, makes it difficult to verify many of the claims made by Gardner and other early Wiccans. Furthermore, there was often a desire among occultists to create a mystique about themselves

Fortunately, we can learn a great deal about Wicca by looking at the rituals, practices and beliefs of the early Wiccans and the early writings of Gardner and other prominent members, such as the following:

Doreen Valiente, who re-wrote many of Gardner's writings, giving them a poetic quality, was probably the most influential woman in early Wicca and was a member of both Gardnerian and Cochranian covens. Among her most important works are: "Where Witchcraft Lives" (1962); "An ABC of Witchcraft" (1973); "Natural Magic" (1975); "Witchcraft for Tomorrow" (1978); and "The Rebirth of Witchcraft" (1989).

Patricia Crowther was initiated by Gerald Gardner. Among her most significant books are: "The Witches Speak" (1965); Witchcraft in Yorkshire"(1973); "Witch Blood: The Diary of a Witch High Priestess" (1974); and "Lid Off the Cauldron: A Handbook for Witches" (1981).

Of course, one of the best sources of information is the writings of Gerald Gardner. The most important of these are: "High Magic's Aid" (1949); "Witchcraft Today" (1954); and "The Meaning of Witchcraft" (1959).

Because of the similarity of the Wiccan ritual of casting a circle to the Lesser Banishing Ritual of the Pentagram, there is speculation that it was derived from the rituals of the Hermetic Order of the Golden Dawn or a similar organization, such as the Rosicrucians or the Ordo Templi Orientis.

A major influence on early Wicca was the work of an Egyptian anthropologist, Margaret Alice Murray, who wrote "The Witch Cult in Western Europe: A Study in Anthropology," first published in 1921, which put forth the hypothesis of a pagan resistance to Christianity in Europe. Her later book, "The God of the Witches," first published in 1931, stated that witches were survivors of an ancient pagan religion, which had remained underground under the onslaught of Christian domination and persecution. Murray's theories were not well-supported by many of her peers.

Although evidence for the assertion that a form of pagan worship had been driven underground, yet survived, appears to be evidenced by another major influence on early Wicca, a book by the English folklorist Charles Leland entitled, "The Gospel of Aradia," first published in 1899, which purports to be an account of the practice of late 19th century Italian witches.

Other influences on Wicca were closer to home and involved Celtic deities and old Irish folklore. It seems that, from the beginning, Wicca was an eclectic belief system, assembled from an assortment of myths, legends and ceremonial magic practices. The early Wiccans' claim of being the modern incarnation of an ancient pagan-witch cult may not be wholly without merit, although it certainly lacks much concrete support.

## Neo-Wicca

Wicca is said to have formally arrived in the U.S. in 1972 with the publication of Raymond Buckland's first book entirely devoted to the subject, entitled "Witchcraft from the Inside." This advent sparked the rise of American Wicca or what is sometimes called neo-Wicca because it is considerably more independent and less formally organized than the original form, which is now referred to as British Traditional Wicca.

This fact may well be due to some of Bucklands' writings, such as "Practical Candleburning Rituals," published in 1970 and "Buckland's Complete Book of Witchcraft," published in 1986, which encouraged the solitary practice of Wicca. Buckland is an Englishman, a Gardnerian initiate, the founder of Seax-Wica, and a prolific author, who came to the U.S. in 1962. (www.raybuckland.org)

Americans were not entirely unfamiliar with Wicca by the 1960s, partly because of the popularity of British-born immigrants like Sybil Leek and Paul Huson who had a big influence on American occult literature. Both authors were familiar with Wicca from their native land, but they rejected it.

Sybil Leek was particularly opposed to certain Wiccan principles, such as the practice of nudity and the prohibition of black magic. Paul Huson's excellent book, "The Mastery of Witchcraft," appears to be the basis for director George A. Romero's movie, "Season of the Witch," (alternatively titled "Hungry Wives") released in 1972, which accurately reflects the role of witchcraft among some women in suburbia in that era of social upheaval.

During the 1970s, Wicca underwent dramatic changes. This was especially true in the U.S., where witchcraft, on the whole, gained unprecedented popularity during the early years of the women's movement. Wicca, which was initially founded by men, was taken up by women who formed covens comprised entirely of women, in which men were either excluded or employed only ceremonially. This new variation was called Dianic Wicca.

The most influential Wiccan of this movement was Z. Budapest, who is the founder and High Priestess of the first feminist, women-only coven, called the Susan B. Anthony Coven #1. She is credited with founding the Women's Spirituality Movement in the U.S. as well as being a powerful secular proponent of human rights for women. (www.zbudapest.com)

In 1979, a journalist named Margot Adler authored "Drawing Down the Moon," which told the story of Wicca from its origins up to that time in an objective, journalistic style. For many new Wiccans, this book was their introduction to Wicca and neo-paganism. This important book was revised and re-released in 2006.

By the 1980s, Wicca was very different from how it was before the 1970s. In fact, the state of contemporary Wicca was such that modern adherents would likely be appalled at some of the practices of the earlier Wiccans, such as the Gardnerian initiation ceremony described by Patricia Crowther in "Witch Blood," wherein she is led around the circle by Gardner like a dog on a leash. In the 1950s and the early 1960s, Wicca was very male dominated and women were expected to obey their masters.

To get an idea of what early Wicca was like, see the 1964 documentary, "Legend of the Witches," directed by Malcolm Leigh. Alexander Sanders of the Alexandrian Tradition contributed heavily to this film, which includes the sacrifice of an animal for divination purposes and features coven members performing rituals that look and sound vaguely Catholic, except for the nudity and bondage.

A central tenet of modern Wicca, known as the Wiccan Rede was established fairly late in the religion's development. The Rede, which is a guideline for living and the closest thing to a commandment, emerged and became a widespread feature of Wicca. In variations on the following eight words, it counsels adherents, "'An it harm none, do as thou wilt." The origin of this admonishment is cloudy, although the Wiccan Rede may have been "derived from something inspired by Valiente's speech in 1964."[1]

It is important to note that the Wiccan Rede bears a striking resemblance to the esoteric scientific principle, eloquently stated by Aleister Crowley in "The Book of the Law" (also, titled "Liber AL vel Legis"), first published in 1904, wherein he states, "Love is the law, love under will" and "Do as thou wilt shall be the whole of the law."

Most modern Wiccans adhere to the Wiccan Rede. Although strict Gardenerians do not and defer all matters of morality to the goddess herself based on a portion of Gerald Gardner's "Gardnerian Book of Shadows," first published in 1957, called, "The Charge of the Goddess." It states, "For my Law is Love unto all beings. 'Keep pure your highest ideals. Strive ever towards it. Let naught stop you or turn you aside.'"2

By 1970, the Three Fold Law of Returns was introduced into contemporary Wicca by Raymond Buckland in his book, "Witchcraft Ancient and Modern" Now widely accepted by Wiccans, this law states that whatever you do will come back to you three times.

Innumerable covens and other organizations grew out of the original Wicca from Britain and developed on both sides of the Atlantic. Their numbers are in constant flux as they are very independent and such organizations form and dissolve all the time. Wiccan authors have written books espousing their own variations on Wicca and even dividing it into previously unimaginable categories, such as Wicca for teens, Wicca for college students, Wicca for the urban dweller, Gothic Wicca and applying the Wiccan construct to a variety of "traditions" creating such variations as the Slavic, Nordic, Gypsy, American Indian, Fairy, and even Christian Wicca.

In some places, Wicca has become a mainstream religion, propelled by events in the worlds of publishing and film that brought this benign, benevolent form of nature worship to the surface of popular culture. In the 1990s, a major New Age publishing house named Llewellyn, which previously had remained fairly obscure, suddenly began to take up most of the space on bookshelves in the New Age section of mainstream bookstores.

In the late 1980s and early '90s, because of movies, like "Practical Magic" (1988) and "The Craft" (1996), the regular meetings of witches were crashed by hordes of high school and college students eager to know more about "the craft." Their heads were filled with fanciful, erroneous ideas from these movies, which they had already come to accept as truth.

As Wicca became a fad among these young people and in those years, it began to change drastically, again, so that many of its new, young members can barely recognize the Wicca of only 30 years ago.

During this time, the Wiccan Rede came to be seen as more of a law than a guideline by many. Buckland's Three Fold Law of Returns seemed to emerge from the shadows as a new dogma, commonly referred to as "karmic law." Only, now, it was modified to state that whatever you do will come back to you seven times, nine times, and so on.

Wicca began to move away from the feminist, entirely goddess-centered religion of the 1970s to a more balanced and inclusive version. Eventually, Wiccans, also, began to acquire new beliefs from the burgeoning self-help and positive thinking movements.

Wicca has become a mainstream cultural phenomenon. It seems reactionary to Christianity and the status quo, but this is only on the surface. It has a lot in common with Christianity, which is why people who are looking for an alternative religion often discover, in a short time, that Wicca is very much a proponent of the status quo.

## CHAPTER 3
## HOW DO PEOPLE BECOME WICCANS?

Increasing numbers of people are born into Wiccan families and grow up practicing Wicca. But even more people choose to become Wiccan at some point in their lives.

Most Wiccans and other types of witches, as well, are solitary practitioners. The biggest benefit of this is that your course of study and the pace at which you do it is entirely self-determined.

In order to be considered a true Wiccan, you must receive an initiation in which you ritualistically renounce your past life and dedicate yourself to Wicca. There are simple initiation rituals you can conduct for yourself. This can be a very important psychological step for people who are deprogramming after coming in contact with Christianity.

"Buckland's Complete Book of Witchcraft" gives initiations for both covens and solitary practitioners. Doreen Valiente's "Witchcraft for Tomorrow" answers a lot of questions about becoming a Wiccan, including initiation. Two more very popular books for solitary Wiccans are: "Solitary Witch: The Ultimate Book of Shadows for the New Generation" by Silver Ravenwolf and "Wicca: A Guide for the Solitary Practitioner" by Scott Cunningham.

Solitary practitioners, also, sometimes participate in open circles. These are not covens, but often extensions of a study group or they may be regularly scheduled, informal meetings associated with a group of neo-pagans.

Many Wiccans desire to join a coven, however, this is not something you should seriously consider until you have studied on your own for some time. A good reason for studying for a while before you do this is to make sure you have a clear understanding of what Wicca is and isn't, so you will not be led astray by anyone.

Covens consist of no more than 13 people including the high priest or high priestess. Many successful covens are much smaller, consisting of only 3 or 4 people who have a commonality of purpose. Sometimes two or more friends who share a common interest in witchcraft decide to form a coven of their own. These organic groupings are often the most sincere, cohesive and successful ones.

In the case of formally established covens, members are usually selected from people who attend their study groups and then only after the other members get to know you. You will certainly want to take the time to get to know them, as well. Like other initiation-based organizations, Wiccan covens typically have an outer circle and one or more inner circles. If you are admitted to an established coven, there will be a formal initiation ritual conducted by the high priest or high priestess.

A good way to find a prospective coven is to first locate a Wiccan study group at your local metaphysical bookstore or online at a source such as Witch Vox (www.witchvox.com). If you have the opportunity, attend other kinds of Wiccan or neo-pagan gatherings or festivals like Pagan Pride Day. Talk to people. Tell them what your interests are and ask them polite questions.

When you find an organization that interests you, spend some time looking at their web site or any other information you can find about them. Most Wiccan groups are not more than 40-years old in the U.S. and about 60-years old in the U.K, but try to find one that has been established for more than just a few years.

Learn as much as you can about the organization before approaching them. If possible, locate a calendar of events and look a their schedule to decide if it is compatible with your own. Look at a map and see how conveniently located they are in relation to your work place or home. Look to see if they accept new members. Many do not and most are by invitation only. Give consideration to their particular tradition and by laws. Determine such things as if they practice skyclad or not and whether or not they appear child-friendly.

This last consideration could affect your satisfaction with the group whether you have children or not. Depending on your situation, a child-friendly group could be either beneficial or unacceptable. Also, as a general rule for your own protection, do not join a coven that engages in skyclad rituals with children present, which could definitely be construed as illegal. Most responsible covens do not permit members under the age of 18.

Gather as much information as you can about a particular coven before contacting the leader. When you first speak to their representative, make an effort to appear organized and professional. Tell them you might be interested in learning more about their organization and ask if they are accepting members at this time. Have a list of relevant questions at hand and be prepared to explain why you want to join a coven and what you feel you could bring to the group.

Typically, people join a coven because they feel they have learned as much as they can on their own and they are looking for guidance. Often, they are looking for camaraderie and fellowship, although this can be found simply by attending events, meetings and study groups. Covens provide a closer, more cohesive relationship, which requires that people know each other well and have a high level of trust.

Participating in a coven can be time-consuming, and it is usually not free. You may be required to have certain clothing and tools, some of which may be expensive. Therefore, before you commit your energy and your mind to something that is potentially going to affect your relationships, your thoughts and your actions, take the time to look at it very closely and determine if it is right for you. If you are asked to take some kind of oath, consider any possible implications of this before agreeing to do so.

When you make first contact with a new group of people, use discretion for the sake of your personal safety. There is an all too common tendency, especially among young neo-pagans, to assume that those who share their interest have intentions as well-meaning as their own.

Do not give too many details about your residence, school, work place or your habits. There is no need for you to use your real name, either. While this may sound paranoid, these are the words of experience. Please, consider them accordingly.

At this point, it is incumbent upon the author to warn newcomers with regard to the nature of some unscrupulous religious leaders who prey upon neo-pagans by forming covens in an attempt to lure unsuspecting people for the purpose of satisfying their own sexual depravity. Women who have recently left a patriarchal religion and have little or no familiarity with neo-pagan religions can too easily fall prey to them. Even long-time practitioners can be taken by surprise by such people, who pose as leaders of pagan or Wiccan groups. These are usually men who see pagan women as easy marks.

It has happened that such people have tried to recruit members by networking online and through metaphysical bookstores. They exploit the Great Rite and other aspects of neo-paganism to sexually and spiritually abuse women and others. There are some other ostensibly neo-pagan groups that exist mainly as sex parties and regularly conduct orgies at sabbats and esbats.

It is true that pagans, in general, have far less restrictive views on sexual behavior than many mainstream Americans or Britons, but it is important that such activities take place between consenting adults. The problem comes when predators falsely represent themselves as spiritual leaders in an attempt to lure victims or employ coercion. This is something to be aware of when you are investigating any group you've seen advertised anywhere.

Consider the fact that most churches are begun by men who, although they may be sincerely religious, are interested in acquiring power, adulation and money. Organized religion is fundamentally a mechanism to control other people's minds and bodies and make money while doing so. Some pagan religious leaders are no different.

It's a case for getting a couple of close friends together for a regular study group and starting your own coven, so you don't run up against this kind of thing.

Keep in mind that Wicca is only one aspect of neo-paganism, one tiny aspect of witchcraft and but a mere fragment of the study of the occult. If you are shopping for an occult religion or philosophy, you would be wise to look at the wide variety of other options available to you before you commit yourself to anything.

# CHAPTER 4
# THE ATTRACTION OF WICCA

Wicca has been made to appear very glamorous in movies and on television, which remain the means by which many people have knowledge of the subject. This characterization of witches, together with the public expounding by prominent Wiccans on the fact that Wicca is a benign nature religion, has helped to make it the most acceptable form of witchcraft. Furthermore, it has become highly accessible, with numerous books on the subject appearing on the shelves of major book retailers.

Wicca is attractive, in part, because it is an acknowledged religion, which provides some legal protections witches have never had before. Being part of a religion grants members a preferred status over that of people who do not have a religious affiliation. Any activity or philosophy that is backed up by the status of being a religion is generally held in higher esteem, especially by other religious people.

There are numerous other established neo-pagan religions, but Wicca is the least off-putting to both newcomers and outsiders. Furthermore, it is the brand of witchcraft that has continually received the most attention. Almost everyone has heard of it.

In densely populated areas of the country, you will find that most people have, at least, some knowledge of Wicca, which they have gained from either watching movies or television series, like "Charmed." They, also, get information from modern, television documentaries on witchcraft, which portray Wicca—and only Wicca, as a rule—very positively.

A Wiccan priestess consulted on the film, "The Craft," which has been a major driving force behind the current state of Wicca's popularity. In fact, it has become so popular, and representatives of Wicca have been so vocal in defending it from detractors that, especially in the U.S., many people no longer believe any malefic form of witchcraft exists.

People are drawn to Wicca for a number of reasons, including its reverence for women and the divine feminine principle, its relative simplicity, its respect for nature and for all people regardless of race, sex, sexual orientation and so on.

For many people, it is the first time they have been given permission to be a little more free than they were as Christians. In many ways, Wicca does not differ much from Christianity, so it isn't too uncomfortable for people who are just beginning to deprogram themselves.

Spiritually abused people are often drawn to Wicca. Women, in particular, are drawn to it, as well as men who see a disturbing sex imbalance in the Judeo-Christian-Islamic religion and in the culture as a whole. Wicca can help to heal some of these psychological wounds because it places a great deal of emphasis on honoring the divine principle of the feminine. In Wicca, women are usually the primary spiritual leaders, and the primary deities are feminine. Furthermore, it makes sense to a lot of people that a benevolent creative force would be feminine rather than masculine.

People who have been newly released from the spiritual bondage of patriarchal religion and all of the abuses that go along with it, sometimes become fanatical about the goddess, especially at first. This is part of the healing process. This is especially true for women because we live in a culture where violence is almost as much a part of living as breathing is for many, if not most, women and girls. The patriarchy is damaging to men, too, but it is most damaging to women who are the greatest objects of their sexual objectification and hatred.

Understandably, anger toward the patriarchy and patriarchal religions is part of the healing process for the people who have been most severely abused by them. For this reason, many covens are comprised entirely of women. They exclude men because doing so is more beneficial to helping women to heal from their psychological and spiritual wounds.

Things are difficult for women now, but most women were virtual slaves before the 1970s. They were not legally permitted to do many of the things we now take for granted, were barred from many jobs and restricted from higher education. Despite the legislation of improved human rights for women, there are massive inequities in terms of real opportunities because of rampant misogyny and violence. This is why Wicca and witchcraft, in general, are still very popular among women. It is no wonder they take comfort in the many faces of the goddess, whose gentleness and love stand in diametric opposition to the hatred, war-like nature and misogyny of the Judeo-Christian-Islamic male deity.

The highest holiday of the year is Beltane, wherein the consummation of the god and goddess, known as the Great Rite, is celebrated as we go forward into the new year. There are 8 sabbats and 13 esbats celebrating the cycles and the power of the sun and the moon. Whenever possible, ritual celebrations are held outdoors in nature.

Wicca helps heal women from the scars of sexual domination and objectification by the patriarchy, in part, through rituals, which are done skyclad to show freedom from sexual repression. By contrast Christianity and other patriarchal religions abhor not only sexuality but the human body and, in particular, women's bodies. Many Christian and Muslim women are expected to cover themselves. So, in Wicca, the beauty and goodness of the human body is emphasized by performing many of their rituals sky-clad. The therapeutic value of this to people trying to break free from the Christian patriarchy is readily apparent.

Some time in the late 1980s and early '90s a little more emphasis began to be placed on the Great Horned God aspect of Wicca. A few covens began to emerge that were comprised mostly or exclusively of gay men who are, also, severely spiritually and psychologically abused by patriarchal religion and the broader society, in general. The author Christopher Penczak has been at the fore of this particular movement with his numerous books on Wicca, which added a much needed fresh perspective to the existing body of work.

A number of Wiccan and neo-pagan covens for men only have sprung up in San Francisco and other large cities. Notable organizations are the Radical Faeries, who are neo-pagans and The Minoan Brotherhood, which is a Wiccan group. The latter has a counterpart for lesbians called the Minoan Sisterhood.

Wiccans typically believe in reincarnation. Many people find the idea of reincarnation comforting or appealing, however, it is especially attractive to people who feel that they have memories of past incarnations.

Newcomers are often attracted by the relative simplicity of Wicca and the positive outlook on life it presents. Wiccans celebrate this life, rather than looking through a sad veil of tears to a heavenly life after death. They do not shun the things that make life full and rich. They enjoy a romantic outlook on nature often applying a characterization of consciousness and wisdom to things in the environment such as trees, animals, streams, and forests.

All rituals or magical workings performed by Wiccans are done with a positive intention. The purpose of many Wiccan rituals is to bring healing and harmony to the world and everything in it. Wiccans have reverence for nature and a love for animals and all living things. Many choose to be vegans, vegetarians or modified vegetarians for this reason alone.

Generally speaking, Wiccans are very peaceful people who seek to find common ground, understanding and tolerance with others. They often look for a peaceful resolution to a conflict and dislike disharmony and violence. They have an egalitarian view of the world and very often they are the peacemakers in the room.

This is very attractive to many people because we live in a world full of disharmony and imbalance in the form of wars, disease, intolerance and tyranny, which is very much in need of peace and healing.

Furthermore, Wicca, especially neo-Wicca, is very flexible. It can be practiced alone, within a family or within a coven.

This is why people who are looking for a religion sometimes find everything they want in Wicca and stay with it for the rest of their lives They find friends and fellowship and a way of looking at the world that makes life more pleasant—more magical. Others stay in Wicca for a while. For many women, it may be a long while as they work out the devastation they have suffered under the patriarchy.

# CHAPTER 5
# BENEFITS OF WICCA

Wicca is a psychologically safe haven from which people, who are new to the occult and might otherwise feel uncertain about it, can explore different ideas while maintaining the safety net of belonging to a religion, complete with behavioral restrictions and social mores. Wicca can provide the necessary grounding for people who have been spiritually abused and frightened by the things they were taught while in the clutches of Christian mind control programmers.

Because Wicca is very flexible, it can be practiced alone or with others and can be used as the framework to study a variety of different traditions. As a result, Wiccans often become surprisingly knowledgeable about particular pantheons of gods and certain aspects of history.

Many Wiccan organizations provide similar benefits to their members and their communities as some churches do. They provide a place for people with similar interests and beliefs to engage in fellowship, participate in study groups and do charity work.

Wiccan leaders, also, perform hand fasting ceremonies, which are weddings usually contracted for a number of months or years. Sometimes coven leaders officiate at funerals, too.

## How Wicca Benefits All of Us

The main benefit of Wicca to all witches is that it has become an officially recognized religion. As such, it has cast an air of legitimacy on all practices of witchcraft by extension. The fact that Wicca has been repeatedly acknowledged as a religion in the U.S., by numerous Supreme Court rulings and defended by respected lawyers like those at the American Civil Liberties Union (ACLU), gives us all a little more protection under the law.[3]

Whenever something negative about witches, in general, is portrayed in the media, it is Wiccans who step forth to defend us all. This is a tremendous benefit because many people in the mainstream are only familiar with Wicca and all they know about it they learned from television and movies. This fact provides a buffer against discrimination and intolerance.

Largely due to the efforts of these highly vocal Wiccans, many people believe that all witches are Wiccans and there is usually no need to disillusion them.

In this way, the Wiccan religion benefits us all. Because of the level of legitimacy Wiccans have achieved, all witches have greater legal protections and are, at least, a little more free to be themselves in public.

# CHAPTER 6
# WHY WICCA IS REJECTED BY MANY OCCULTISTS

Many people who take up the study of Wicca, initially feel a sense of resonance with it and begin calling themselves Wiccans. But, after they study it in depth, more often than not, they come away dissatisfied with it because there is a great deal about it that seems dubious and they do not feel any greater sense of power for having become Wiccan. Sometimes they feel that Wicca is restricting them, although they are not sure why they feel that way when they initially found Wicca to be very liberating.

Many people enjoy a feeling of euphoria upon first discovering Wicca. They become enamored with some aspects of it, usually the goddess, the mythology, and the relative freedom it seems to offer. But, as they encounter the Rede and the Law of Returns and perhaps begin fellowshipping with other Wiccans, they begin to feel somewhat oppressed by it.

That's because Wicca is fundamentally a religion and an increasingly dogmatic and judgmental one. Furthermore, it is the nature of religion to override the interests and the personality of the individual and subordinate it to the ideology of the group.

Religion is a fundamental part of the slave grid, the mind control mechanism of the ancient Babylonian system. It is and always has been the enemy to free thought and freedom itself.

It's not that there aren't important truths in all religions or that they should be entirely avoided. You can learn a great deal from a religion, however, it is important not to cede your mind and personality to it in the course of studying it.

Despite the fact that it is comprised of some probably valid components, Wicca is as much a fraud as any other supposedly legitimate religion. Scientology, Mormonism, the Jehovah's Witnesses and even the oldest religions are all based on unsubstantiated and even outright false or absurd claims. Wicca is by no means unique in that regard.

Yet, many people reject Wicca not for what it is, but what it has become. As they have added new rules to their dogma and acquired new converts, many of whom are fresh from Christianity, many Wiccans have become as intolerant and finger-wagging as any Evangelical.

## Wicca is Susceptible to Popular Social Trends

Even now, modern Wicca is in a state of evolution. In the past several years, it has begun to merge with new elements, which are a combination of psychology, self-help, the positive thinking movement, and the prosperity movement. Many Wiccans have latched onto these popular ideas without bothering to examine them.

The power of positive thinking and the prosperity movement stemmed from some writers of the New Thought Movement of the early 20th century. Its proponents, like William Walker Atkinson, were influenced by Mary Baker Eddy of Christian Science. It is associated with, at least, two well-known fringe Christian churches: Science of Mind and Unity Church. But, many of their ideas began entering the secular world about 100 years ago.

Atkinson wrote the "Law of Attraction in Thought Vibration or The Law of Attraction in the Thought World," in 1908. It was a treatise on how to be successful at business, keep a healthy mental outlook and get along with other people. After the publication of this book, a number of similar ones were published by such authors as Wallace Wattles, Napoleon Hill, and others who combined New Thought ideas with elements from hypnosis, in particular, the work of Emile Coue, who coined the phrase, "Every day, in every way, I'm getting better and better."

Because of its connection with, or rather its confusion with, the esoteric concept of thought forms or mental frequencies, the "Law of Attraction" was taken completely out of context and misapplied by later New Thought writers.

The primary misconceptions among them are that thoughts are literally things and that "like attracts like," which is completely contrary to the most basic occult scientific principles and conventional science, as well. In the world of orthodox science, opposites attract; and in the world of occult science this principle is what makes possible the existence of anything whatsoever on any plane, whether physical or metaphysical.

Similarly, there is a principle in homeopathy, attributed to Samuel Hahnemann, which says "Like cures like," but this, too, is an over-simplification of a more complex concept and is not meant to be taken literally, as it so often is.

Examples of abuses of these esoteric concepts may be found in works by prominent positive thinking gurus from the 1980s until the present time, such as Dyer, Chopra, and Hay, along with the 2004 movie, "What the Bleep Do We Know?" which perverted occult scientific principles and even tried to pass them off as quantum physics.

By 2006, these twisted and misconstrued notions culminated in the publication of a colorful book called, "The Secret," by Rhonda Byrne, an Australian author who subsequently went on the Oprah Winfrey Show and spread this misinformation about the occult to millions of people. There is a film by the same name that goes with this book that has an eerily Christian feel to it. According to Byrne, whatever situation you have in your life, you attracted it with your thoughts and the images you hold in your mind.

Just as her predecessors had done, the author took complex esoteric concepts, processed them down into something extremely basic and presented them in a way that is palatable to mass consumers who live in a world of sound-bites. It could be characterized as "drive-thru occultism" or "fast food for the soul."

Presently, popular culture is saturated with these ideas. The people who espouse them swear that they are based on ancient laws, despite evidence to the contrary. They are, also, very harmful ideas if taken to an extreme, which zealots inevitably do.

Damage is done, not only to the people who adhere to these absurd, poorly researched ideas, but to the people they come in contact with. Their proponents have gone to the ridiculous extreme of saying that victims of horrific crimes, disease, and natural disasters are responsible for what has happened to them because they had negative thoughts. They blame rape survivors for attracting their rapists. They say that the collective mindset of the Jews caused the Nazis to commit mass genocide against them. Then, as if to compound their cruelty, they tell survivors to take a lesson from the horrors that have befallen them.

All of this can be especially psychologically harmful to victims of violent crimes, who are commonly blamed by everyone from family to law enforcement. The callous victim-blaming of these pathological narcissists is spiritual abuse at its worst, all done at the expense of genuine occultism and without the benefit of a Bible, Koran, or Talmud.

Many of these distorted concepts found their way into television, movies, and other aspects of popular culture, which is the same place many Wiccans first come in contact with Wicca. So, the merger of these ideas from recent years together with the Wiccan Rede and the now multiple-fold Law of Returns was practically a fait accompli.

In the last decade or so, their willingness to live in such an upside down and backwards state of unreality along with their naive optimism has earned Wiccans such derisive epithets as "fluffy bunnies" and "white lighters."

## Other Common Criticisms

Another common criticism of Wiccans is that they are often guilty of poor scholarship, knowing little about the origins of Wicca and nothing whatsoever about other forms of witchcraft. Sometimes they will even refuse to acknowledge the existence of other occult practices, even when confronted with them.

While they may find their attitude a little frustrating, most traditional witches are happy to leave Wiccans to their delusions because their mistaken, but sincerely held beliefs, provide a buffer between them and members of the religious establishment who might do them even greater harm if they knew the truth.

A major reason many occultists immediately reject Wicca is that they simply see it as a re-packaged form of Christianity. Wicca is a neutered form of witchcraft that is very similar to liberal Christianity. The free will of the person who gives his or her mind to either is subverted and subordinated to a group mind, an alien ideology.

Wiccans sometimes argue that their religion is superior because while the Christians have their Ten Commandments, Wiccans have only one simple rule, the Rede. This is tantamount to saying, "I am living in a freer prison because it has only one cell, whereas my neighbor's prison is less free because it has ten." Regardless, both are a prison for the mind. Both are oppressive. Both can be spiritually damaging.

A further problem with this single prison cell, the Rede, is that it becomes tantamount to the Christian admonition to "turn the other cheek." It prevents people from doing harm to others in cases where self-defense is necessary, even in cases where they have been severely wronged and justice has been denied. The most offensive thing a Wiccan is permitted to do to anyone is "bind" them from doing harm, a concept made popular among neo-Wiccans by the 1996 movie, "The Craft."

Of course, Gardnerian Wiccans do not acknowledge the Rede, but are bound by the Charge of the Goddess. Although it may be a more lenient one, this is still a restraint placed on the mind and the true will of the individual by a presumably superior ideology.

From an esoteric scientific perspective, the Wiccan religion is problematic because it is obsessed with symbolism without ever arriving at the purpose of those symbols—except to lead to yet another symbol. In this way, it is very circular and monotonous. It is obsessed with sexual relationships, mistaking the corresponding symbolism as a social statement and failing to understand the esoteric science behind it. It seems as if the adherents have become so enmeshed in ritualized celebration that they have entirely lost the deeper meaning of it all.

People reject Wicca for the same reason they reject religion, in general. In the end, they realize that it is just another artificial construct and conclude that, as such, it is an unnecessary limitation.

Furthermore, Wicca is only a very small part of the world of the occult. There is so much more to explore.

# CHAPTER 7
# NON-WICCAN RELIGIONS, ORGANIZATIONS AND PHILOSOPHIES

Paganism itself is not a religion, but there are a quite a few neo-pagan religions that have been formed in recent decades. Unlike Wicca, most of them are not well known. Even though they may fit the modern definition of a religion, some of these are well-organized efforts, and others are less so. They typically incorporate some ceremonial magic tradition, but most have little in common with modern Wicca apart from that.

In general, occultists are very open to other people regardless of sex, sexual orientation, race, nationality or other individual traits. This is not a property unique to Wicca. The inclusion of women on equal footing with men was part of the original tenets of Theosophy and the Golden Dawn, which are the organizations foundational to the entire modern occult movement.

The following are only a few of the most notable non-Wiccan religions, organizations and philosophies. There are too many to acknowledge and many others that are not public.

## Germanic Occultism

German occultism includes a variety of philosophies and a number of organizations. The term, "German," is used here to include Norse, Icelandic, Scandinavian, German, and German-Austrian rooted concepts.

Asatru is probably the largest and best-known German occult

organization. The Asatru are true to the old race of ancestral Germanic gods called the Aesir. It is a polytheistic religion in which the central deity is the All Father, Odin, but they acknowledge the entire ancient German pantheon. Asatru is a reconstructionist, neo-pagan religion.

Typically, members are very scholarly and knowledgeable about the surviving works surrounding the foundation of Asatru, such as, "The Nibelungenlied," "The Eddas," "The Heimskringla" and others. Many surviving documents were preserved from the effects of Christian tyranny, largely in Iceland by Snorri Sturluson and other Medieval scholars. It is not unusual to find Asatru members who speak multiple languages, especially German, Icelandic, Old Norse, or Old Anglo-Saxon.

The closest thing to a rule book for moral conduct in German lore is "The Havamal," from the 13th century "Codex Regius," which offers advice on manners and hospitality. There is an element of magic in Asatru, particularly centering on the esoteric use of the runes and the shamanism of Odin.

The Asatru are frequently in the position of defending themselves from those who confuse their practices with Wicca, including some misguided Wiccans. Although both are neo-pagan religions with some magical tradition, they are very different from each other. They, also, must frequently reiterate that they are not Satanists or neo-Nazis. There is no Satan in Asatru, and it is open to all people who have an interest in venerating the old gods and learning about the history, literature, language, and folkways of the ancient Germans. See: Asatru Alliance, Inc. (asatru.org.)

Besides Asatru, there are numerous similar reconstructionist groups, which include Theodism, Forn Sidr, Foreningen, Forn Sed (recognized as a religion in Norway), Odinism or Wotanism, and Irminism, which is derived from Armanism.

The Austrian occultist Guido von List is one of the most important early figures in the foundation of modern Germanic mysticism and the study of rune lore. He was the founder of the philosophy of Armanism and the author of "Das Geheimnis der Runen" ("The Secret of the Runes"), which is a detailed study of the Armanen Futhark (or ancient German "alphabet") and its uses among the early Germanic tribes. Like many other 19th-century occultists, he was strongly influenced by the work of Madame Blavatsky and the Theosophists.

One of the most important living authors on this subject is Stephen Flowers, whose pen name is Edred Thorsson. Flowers was the first to translate some of List's works, including "The Secret of the Runes," into English.

Some important modern organizations related to Germanic occultism include the Asatru Folk Assembly and the Troth (formerly The Ring of Troth).

Dr. Joseph P. Farrell has done some very impressive scholarly research on the relationship between ancient Germanic occultism and the esoteric science behind Nazi inventions. He appears at U.F.O. conferences to discuss the relationship between German occultism and alternative science, including free energy and flying saucer technology. Among his many fascinating books, "Reich of the Black Sun" and "The Nazi Bell," will be very interesting reading for any occultists, but especially those familiar with German occultism.

The hollow earth theory is a matter related to German folklore that figures heavily into German occultism. It reaches far into its Indo-European roots making a connection, once again, with the work of Madame Blavatsky and the Theosophists.

## Satanism

In modern occultism, the term, "Satanism," is sometimes used to refer to a variety of religions and philosophies including Gnosticism, Luciferianism, and modern Satanism because of their adversarial position to the religious and cultural status quo.

Generally speaking, Satanists do not worship Satan or any other entity. Some are theists, but many are atheists, who do not believe in an anthropomorphic god. Many modern Satanists take an adversarial position toward the status quo by questioning authority.

Satanists are often, also, demonologists, conjurers, and necromancers. They do not worship the devil or demonic entities, although calling one another "devil worshippers" is sometimes an inside joke intended to poke fun at outsiders' false assumptions.

Satanists usually have a disdain for social convention and work to break the mind control programming of the masses. They despise hypocrisy and value individuality. They are not aggressive, but may respond very negatively if they are attacked and they have no moral opposition to the use of black magic. They sometimes engage in controversial or commonly misunderstood practices, such as tantric magic.

As such, they are considered practitioners of the Left Hand Path. This differentiates them from practitioners of the Right Hand Path, who focus on belonging, adherence to social norms, and a conventional moral code.

There are some misguided people involved in Satanism just as there are with other types of organizations, including Christianity and Wicca.

Consider, too, that an aspect of an organization may be legitimate, but it may, also, be a cover for some insidious activities. Like Wicca, other initiatory groups generally have an outer circle and one or more inner ones. The outer circle may be benevolent and charitable, but at the inner core may be an organization of a different nature that has a different agenda.

Therefore, you will want to make a thorough investigation before you decide to join a group. Although it is not necessary to join any organization to be a Satanist.

The best-known Satanic organization in the U.S. is the Church of Satan.

## The Church of Satan

The Church of Satan was officially founded on Walpurgisnacht (Beltane) in 1966 ("the year one") in San Francisco, California, by Anton Szandor LaVey. It is the first organization of its kind to come before the public eye.

Although they are adamant about the fact that they are not humanists, the Church of Satan emphasizes the importance of the individual. It gives people permission to be free, independent and to express themselves fully as natural beings. This message is especially important for many young people who are subjected to the prison-training of the public educational system, therefore, Satanism often has a special appeal to them.

LaVey's Satanism has almost nothing in common with Wicca except that it, too, has been a catalyst for awakening many people to the occult and helping to put them on a path to discovering their own unique identities.

The Church remains a source of fascination to many people, including non-occultists, because LaVey was such a colorful and enigmatic character. He had ties with a number of celebrities, although the truth about many aspects of his life remains a mystery. Of course, most practitioners of the Dark Arts are discreet about what they really do.

One way to learn about LaVey's Satanism is through his work. The first book many people read is "The Satanic Bible," which was first published in 1969 by Avon. It includes the basic tenets of LaVey's Church of Satan, as well as his observations about Satanism and descriptions of Satanic rituals.

You can learn something about Anton LaVey from his own words, immortalized in "Satanis: The Devil's Mass" (1970), which is a documentary on The Church of Satan, starring Anton LaVey, directed and produced by Ray Laurent.

LaVey's daughter, Zeena LaVey Schreck, appeared on numerous talk shows in the 1980s and '90s during what was known as the Satanic Panic. She was a spokesman for The Church of Satan and defended Satanism against false charges by some Christians. At this time, numerous Christian religious leaders wrote books and went on television making false claims about Satanism, which included bringing forth people who falsely claimed to have been involved in Satanic Ritual Abuse. They were eventually exposed and discredited for these ludicrous claims, largely due to the efforts of Zeena LaVey.

She is currently the spiritual leader of the Sethian Liberation Movement, which according to an interview with Ms. Schreck, involves practices similar to those of the Hindu siddhas, including shape shifting through meditation.[4]

Anton LaVey passed on in 1997. The current leader of The Church of Satan is Blanche Barton, who has, also, written the definitive biography of Anton LaVey, entitled "The Secret Life Of A Satanist: The Authorized Biography of Anton LaVey" and "The Church of Satan: A History of the World's Most Notorious Religion," both published in 1990. The Church of Satan is currently headquartered in New York City. It has two different types of memberships, which are explained at their official web site. (www.churchofsatan.org)

On October 31, 1999, Anton LaVey's eldest daughter, Karla, founded The First Church of Satan, which she feels is a nearer representation to her father's original organization. It is currently headquartered in San Francisco. (www.satanicchurch.com)

## The Temple of Set

If there is any Satanic figure more interesting than Anton LaVey, it would have to be Lt. Col. Michael Aquino, the high ranking military man whose name was often heard on the nightly news during the 1980s in connection with the Ronald Reagan administration. He is a former member of the Church of Satan, who split with LaVey and founded his own Satanic organization, the Temple of Set.

Because of Aquino, Satanism has a small degree of acceptance as a religion in the U.S. military. The Temple of Set places an emphasis on esoteric science and its application. Its membership rolls are filled with prominent names in higher education and government.

Aquino was personally swept up into the Satanic Panic and while many of the claims against him seem obviously false, some others definitely raise an eyebrow.

Nebraska Senator John DeCamp, who authored the book, "The Franklin Cover Up," about orphan children, who were supplied as sex slaves to high ranking members of the U.S. government, fingered Aquino as a key figure in this pedophile ring.[5]

Aquino is, also, mentioned several times, in the context of the MK-Ultra Mind Control project, in the book, "Trance Formation of America," by Cathy O'Brien, in which she describes Aquino as a hypnotist with remarkable abilities, whose expertise was used in black operations within the U.S. Government that went all the way to the White House.[6] (www.trance-formation.com)

There is little doubt from Aquino's own writings, such as "From PSYOP to MindWar: The Psychology of Victory" by Col. Paul E. Valley with Major Michael Aquino, available at the Temple of Set web site, that he was involved in Psychological Operations (Psy Ops).[7]

Governments have always used occultists, astrologers, and sorcerers, at least, as far back as Queen Elizabeth I, if not to the days of King Arthur's court. They were, also, widely used by the old Soviet KGB and by the CIA and British Secret Intelligence Services (SIS, also, known as M16).

Other prominent occultists alleged to have worked for the British or American governments include Aleister Crowley, Dion Fortune, and Sybil Leek, just to name a few. Dion Fortune documents the use of magic in the defense of Britain during World War II in her book entitled, "The Magical Battle of Britain."

The best place to learn more about the Temple of Set is at their own web site. (www.xeper.org)

## Who is Satan?

Although Satanists do not believe in or worship the Judeo-Christian-Islamic entity, Satan, the question of the existence of an entity, called "Satan," is widely discussed.

The words, "Satan," "Satanic," and "Satanism," are controversial and have different meanings to different people.

In common parlance, the term, "Satanic," is sometimes used by people to denote an evil, depraved act. In this case, it is not a reference to the religion or philosophy of Satanism, but is used metaphorically.

On several occasions the term, "Satan," is used in the Old and New Testaments of the Bible to describe a tempting or provoking spirit.

In present-day Christian parlance, "Satan" is used to refer to both a particular entity, who is regarded as an enemy, and as a metaphor for multiple adversarial forces. The term is synonymous with "the devil." In later translations of the Bible, beginning with the one commissioned by the infamous witch hunter, King James I of England, the word, "Satan," is used in passages where the word, "adversary," had previously been.

Of course, from a Christian perspective, all witches are Satanist and all practices not associated with a major world religion that they recognize are considered Satanic. Within Christianity, Satan is the personification of evil. Fallen angels and their demonic minions are collectively referred to by this term, as if they are one entity. Satan is commonly conflated with entities that occultists regard as separate beings with distinct personalities, for example, Lucifer, Asmodeus, and Beliel.

When we try to trace the history of an entity called "Satan," we find mention in the Koran of an adversarial entity with a similar sounding name, "Shaitan," which is Arabic. Here it is a rebellious spirit or jinn. Of course, Christianity and Islam are both offshoots of Judaism.

It is possible that the term, "Satan," entered the Hebrew lexicon during the time of the Babylonian captivity of the Jews in about the 6th century B.C. and that such an entity was already known to people in that region.

In the Old Testament Book of Isaiah 14:12-17, Helel, a Babylonian King and Jewish oppressor, whose name may be translated as "Shining One," is poetically compared to the Morning Star. In the later King James version of this passage, what had been translated as "Morning Star" became "Lucifer."

Lucifer is believed to be a fallen angel who was once a co-creator with God, although in some accounts this God may not be anthropomorphic, but rather an energetic force.

Further evidence to support a connection, although a confused one, between Satan and a Lucifer-like being may be found in a book entitled, "Devil Worship: The Sacred Books and Traditions of the Yezidiz," by Isya Joseph, published in 1919.[8]

The Yezidis (alternately spelled "Yazidis") are Indo-Persians who are likely descendants of the ancient Assyrians. They believe that theirs is the oldest religion and that they were the first people created in the biblical Garden of Eden, which they claim is Lalish in Iraq.

Their beliefs are similar to those of some Gnostics in that they believe the world was created and set in motion by a non-anthropomorphic god, who left seven angels in charge. Chief among these is their Peacock Angel, Melek Ta`us, who fell to earth from heaven.

Their Islamic neighbors have been persecuting them as devil worshippers for centuries because they believe that Melek Ta`us is Azazel, the adversary to their God Allah, which is the same God as that of the Jews and the Father-god of the Christians. According to Islam, Azazel is the original name of Iblis, the angelic spirit who once worshipped their god before his rebellion. Iblis is a jinn that whispers in the ears of men to lead them astray. Incidentally, Azazel is described as a goat-like being in the Jewish Old Testament.

The Yezidi people had, at least at one time, an ancient, mysterious book that was the record of their history. This book may have been the inspiration for H.P. Lovecraft's Cthulu.[9]

Interestingly, there is an initiatory, non-Wiccan, witchcraft cult founded in the U.S. in the 1920s, with roots in both the Golden Dawn, Celtic fairy lore and folk magic from the Ozark mountain region. Feri witchcraft or Vicia centers around an androgynous, blue angel, identified as Melek Ta`us of the Yezidis.

In Egypt, in approximately 1600 B.C., we find another being with a similar name to Satan. "Sata" may be described as "Ouroboros," a dragon eating it's tail. Sata is, also, called "Tuat", and he is the conveyor of the dawn or the morning light, who might be construed as Lucifer.

All over the world at different times in history, there are other entities with similar names and similar relationships to serpents, dragons, flying serpents, or birds clutching serpents going back to the earliest civilization. These things are often associated with the earth and an ancient race of demi-gods or fallen angels. The term, "Satan," had and continues to have diverse meanings. Depending on who uses the term, it may or may not be associated with Lucifer.

## Luciferianism

Modern Western Luciferianism is more often a philosophy than a religion. Sometimes, it bears similarities to Gnosticism. If you ask a Luciferian to explain Luciferianism, you will receive a variety of different and probably very intriguing answers.

Luciferians do not worship Lucifer or any other entity. Lucifer is sometimes associated with the rebellious Greek demi-god Prometheus, who rebelled against Zeus and gave the knowledge of fire to man. Lucifer was an advocate for mankind, not only the literal bringer of the light of dawn, but a bringer of illuminating wisdom. He may be likened to other entities in ancient history and lore.

In the early Sumerian story of the creation of man, there are two figures, Enki and Enlil, who are brothers. Enki and his sister Ninhursag are the co-creators of man, whom they made from their own genetic material combined with that of some other being already on earth. Enki was pleased with his creation, but his brother Enlil was jealous of him and became angry with mankind. He demanded that man worship him and only him as their one and only god. When humans advanced in their knowledge despite his restrictive edicts, he became angry and brought a deluge in an attempt to destroy them.

Enki, the good brother and advocate for man, may be likened to Lucifer. While his wicked brother, who hates man and places all kinds of rules and restraints on him, may be likened to the god of the Jews, Muslims and Christians.

Lucifer is sometimes seen as a co-creator with god, although he later rebelled. He is seen as both a beautiful angel of light in the heavens and as a goat-like creature who represents the earth. Lucifer's symbol is a peacock or a serpent. His name means "light bearer," "morning star," or "bringer of the dawn."

## The Golden Dawn and the Theosophists

The original New Age movement can accurately be described as Luciferian. Its seminal organization is The Hermetic Order of the Golden Dawn. The order's name refers to the dawn of a new age of enlightenment, as we transition from the astrological Age of Pisces to the Age of Aquarius. The original organization, which was established in the late 19th century, is now defunct. But, members of the Golden Dawn left behind a very large body of written works.

At their core, they were a free mason-like organization, heavily influenced by the Rosicrucians. Unlike other orders of its kind, the Golden Dawn admitted women as equal members to men and promoted the brotherhood of all mankind. In further contrast, the purpose of the Golden Dawn was not to hoard information about esoteric science, but to disseminate it in anticipation of the Aquarian Age, in which old, oppressive structures are to be destroyed.

It was, also, heavily influenced by the work of Madame Blavatsky and the Theosophists, who are, also, Luciferian. Helena P. Blavatsky was a Russian mystic who, together with Col. H.S. Olcott, founded the Theosophical Society in England in 1875. Blavatsky's most import works are: "The Secret Doctrine" and "Isis Unveiled." Theosophy was conceived of as a Universal Brotherhood that accepted everyone regardless of race, creed, sex, or social standing.

What became know as the second wave of Theosophy occurred in the early 20th century and included important esoteric scientific works by the authors A.E. Powell, C.W. Leadbeater, and Annie Besant. They created much of the language we used to describe occult concepts today. In the 1920s, the Theosophist Alice Bailey founded the Luciferian

Publishing Company, later known as Lucis Trust Publishing. In 1932, she founded a human rights organization called the World Goodwill Group, known as Lucis Trust Ltd. in the U.K. (www.lucistrust.org)

The work of the French author and ceremonial magician Eliphas Levi was a strong influence on the Golden Dawn and other occultists. Perhaps the most important work by Levi, "Dogma et Rituel," first published in 1854, was translated into English by Arthur Edward Waite and re-titled, "Transcendental Magic, its Doctrine and Ritual."

Francis Barrett's book, "The Magus," along with the work of Queen Elizabeth I's court astrologer, John Dee, concerning Enochian magic, as well as a great number of other grimoires and works by ancient alchemists were influential to the Golden Dawn.

Israel Regardie's works are lessons in the occult, which include ceremonial practices, astrology, the Kabbalah, the tarot, numerology, and other esoteric sciences. Regardie's "A Garden of Pomegranates" is a key book to understanding the Kabbalah. The foundational book for students of the Golden Dawn is "The Golden Dawn: The Original Account of the Teachings, Rites & Ceremonies of the Hermetic Order," which is a lesson book in the study of occultism and ritual magic. After the student is familiar with those books, "The Middle Pillar" and "The Tree of Life" are recommended.

Among the most notable members of the Golden Dawn were Aleister Crowley, Israel Regardie, Dion Fortune, Arthur Edward Waite, S.L. MacGregor Mathers, and William Butler Yeats. Each of these people contributed substantially to the body of work of the Golden Dawn.

## Gnosticism

Little is known about the early Gnostics, who were Christian mystics of the 1st century. The Gnostic Gospels, which comprise over 100 books, were first discovered in Nag Hammadi, Egypt in 1945. They were originally written in Coptic, translated from Biblical era Greek. They have cast a new light on the early, pre-Catholic history of Christianity.

The Greek term, "gnosis," is translated as "knowing," which is seen as the process of obtaining knowledge. To the Gnostics knowledge was to be found within, and it was something that had to be arrived at through a process of meditation and mysticism. It is no wonder that the earliest Christians were mystics, considering that Jesus Christ himself was a magician with powers of healing, levitation, transmutation, prophesy, and the ability to leave the physical plane of existence and return at will.

Gnosticism was one of the early threads of the Christian religion before it was established in Rome in 330 A.D. and evolved into the religious institution we all know today. Even in its present stage of development, Catholicism is a mystical tradition with many practices resembling traditional witchcraft, and remarkable powers are attributed to the saints.

These early Gnostic Christians were regarded as heretical by the dominant faction centered in Rome and many of their writings were destroyed by about the 6th century, after which they sank into obscurity. Some people say they were the true Christians and their form of the religion was closer to how Christianity should be practiced.

The earliest Gnostics were called Simonians after Simon the Magus, the powerful sorcerer whose status as a witch is noted in "Acts 3:9-24." He is, also, mentioned in the "Acts of Peter," "Pseudo-Clementines," and "The Epistle of the Apostles," which are apocryphal works. Simon the Magus was capable of levitation and had the ability to fly at will. He and his followers were said to commit a variety of "sins," including conjuration, casting spells, concocting potions, interpreting dreams, and practicing divination.

The cosmology of Gnosticism is complex. There seems to be no real agreement among Gnostics on many points, however, they mainly assert that the Judeo-Christian story of Genesis has been reversed to confound believers and trick them into worshipping an evil god.

They believe the world was set in motion outside of the duality of time and space, in what would be called the Ayn (Ain) of the Theosophists and the Kabbalists. In Gnosticism, this is called the Pleroma, in which dwell 30 aeons, who could be regarded as gods or a high order of angels.

The goddess Sophia, whose name means "wisdom," created an angel who became the tyrannical creator god of the Old Testament. He was unaware of the power of the benevolent aeons. It was he who made man, but Sophia gave him a soul. Then, against the wishes of their creator, who wanted to keep them in a state of ignorance and enslavement, she sent the serpent, either the angel Samael or Michael, into the Garden of Eden to bestow knowledge upon Adam and Eve by means of the fruit of the tree of knowledge.

In Gnosticism, women are revered. Some Gnostics believe in both a kind of purgatory and reincarnation.

A group of Gnostics, called the Mandaeans, still survives in present-day Iraq and Iran. While they accept the notion of a Messiah, they deny that it was Jesus, but rather John the Baptist.

Since the discovery of the Gnostic Gospels, many ideas from them have found their way into modern occultism. Gnosticism has many things in common with Luciferianism, particularly regarding a similar belief of the Yezidis that their peacock angel, identified with Lucifer, is the true benefactor of mankind.

# CHAPTER 8
# TRADITIONAL WITCHCRAFT

Traditional witchcraft is more often non-religious and generally not well organized. The term encompasses old practices, many of which are taking place right under the noses of the unsuspecting general public, as well as the more exotic forms being practiced around the world. While many people in the last 50 to 100 years have been busy rediscovering witchcraft, the fact is, it has never gone anywhere. It has been right here all along.

Far from being dead, witchcraft is a very old, living practice. It has been especially well preserved in some parts of the U.S. and Mexico that have remained culturally isolated.

Naturally, the oldest occult practices in the United States are those of the American Indians, which were documented by English and Spanish-speaking Europeans who encountered or lived with them in previous centuries.

From these writers, we know that they made use of something like poppet magic in the form of fetishes, to which they offered prayers to ensure a fruitful hunt. They were adept healers, well-versed in the use of medicinal herbs. In fact, a few successful anti-tumor formulas in popular use by herbalists today are derived from their knowledge of the native herbs. They were aware of their relationship to the world of spirits, not only of ancestors but of animals and other non-human entities. The various tribes have many unique and interesting legends.

Despite the efforts of Christian missionaries, this ancient spiritualism is kept alive on reservations and is an important part of life for many modern American Indians. In some areas of the country, they regularly delight audiences with their spirit-evoking dances, which are a part of their ancient pagan practices.

In the relatively short history of the U.S., as those of European descent merged with the Indians, we began to synthesize and absorb each others' ideas about the nature of the world. This is the origin of many beliefs relating to the observation of plants and animals in predicting future events, including the best timing for planting and harvesting. Some of this lore is preserved in "The Old Farmer's Almanacs," which can still be purchased annually, especially in rural parts of the country.

In isolated regions of the U.S., the old witchcraft practices imported from western Europe have continued without much commentary because they are simply part of life. This is the case among some people in the mountainous regions of Appalachia and the Ozarks.

People in the southern Appalachian Mountain region seem to be very conscious of the spirit world and a lot of interesting ghost stories come from this area. Although many are ardent Bible believers and will quickly deny such "superstitious nonsense," others are open to sharing their experiences if you get to know them and express a genuine interest in the subject.

The aspect of Appalachian witchcraft best preserved in print is that of the Pennsylvania Dutch in the book,"Pow-Wows, or, Long Lost Friend," by John George Hohman, which was first published in 1820. It is a collection of folk remedies, spells, and talismans compiled by Hohman, who was an American healer of German descent. The term, "Pow-wow," is taken from the Algonquin word for "medicine men." Evidence of the practice of German witchcraft can be seen today in the protective symbols that are placed on the outside of barns throughout Pennsylvania.

Many native Ozarkers are descendants of the Appalachians, whose ancestors came from Scotland and England. They brought their beliefs with them and preserved old traditions, including particular spells performed on May Day, and spiritual practices involving divining the future and speaking to the spirits of the dead.

For many years, they were cut off from the outer world because of the roughness of the terrain and they were not exposed to popular culture. Ozark culture was documented by Vance Randolph in "Ozark Superstitions," published in 1947, wherein he describes spells, rituals and divination as ordinary practices, woven into the fabric of everyday life, even though most people, also, have a Bible in their homes.

The ease of modern transportation has made these areas more accessible than they were just a few decades ago, but many of the people who live in the region covered in Randolph's book remain the same, isolated, secretive, and suspicious of outsiders. There's every reason to believe that these practices continue unabated, if not encouraged by the renewed popularity of witchcraft.

In the southern regions of the U.S., an entirely different spiritual life is going on to which white southerners remain mostly oblivious. African and Afro-Caribbean spirituality thrives all around the Gulf of Mexico with slight variations.

Voodoo is the best-known variety of Hoodoo, mostly because of old horror movies like "White Zombie," the 1932 movie starring Bela Lugosi. American Voodoo began in New Orleans. But, it is commonly practiced, not just in hubs like southeastern Louisiana and Memphis, Tennessee, but all throughout the south. It is similar to the practice of Vodou in Haiti, but it is only one part of the broader practice of Hoodoo.

In the United States, Hoodoo is a truly American form of witchcraft in that it has synthesized with almost every form of old magical practice that ever existed in the country and its former territories. While it is primarily based in West African spiritual traditions, it is universal in nature, incorporating lost books of the Hebrew Bible, American Indian spiritualism, Santeria, Western grimoires, the Kabbalah, and Western European witchcraft practices. In Hoodoo, portions of the Holy Bible, in particular the Book of Psalms, are used as a powerful grimoire for casting spells.

In the southern states, West African spiritualism, also, merged with Christianity to form Pentecostalism and thus began to influence popular culture through the music of entertainers like Elvis Presley and Jerry Lee Lewis. It influenced both music and dance styles that knocked down cultural walls and helped to free people's minds and bodies. West African spiritualism was a major influence on the soulfully expressive dance style of Isadora Duncan, as well.

One type of Santeria is a synthesis of Catholicism and West African religion, which was created as a result of the Atlantic slave trade. It contains a pantheon of African ancestral deities known as the Orishas. Probably the most famous of these, in American popular culture, is Babalu-Aye, which is, also, the title of a song made famous in the early 1950s by the Cuban-born, American band leader and world-famous comedic actor Desi Arnaz. This call to the Orisha of healing, whose name means "Lord of the Earth," is regularly broadcast all across the nation and around the world in reruns of the television comedy series, "I Love Lucy."

Mexican Santeria is similar, except that the practice revolves more around Roman Catholic-style saints. It includes many saints who are no longer recognized by the Catholic Church and some they regard as purely evil, such as la Santisima Muerte, who is commonly believed to be an ancient Aztec goddess and Jesus Malverde, a legendary Robin Hood-like figure from the State of Sinaloa. Of course, the central saint is Our Lady of Guadalupe, who appears as a manifestation of the goddess Artemis or Diana, often standing on the crescent moon, complete with her consort Lucifer. As Our Lady of Guadalupe, Mother of All, she is not only the central religious figure of Mexican spiritual practice, but represents the national unity of the people of Mexico.

Santeria is a practice common to many Mexicans who are otherwise devout Catholics. It is, also, very common in the U.S., but it is virtually unknown outside regions of the country where Americans of Mexican descent reside. Furthermore, in the areas where there is a large Spanish-speaking population, the language, more often than not, creates a barrier to outsiders obtaining knowledge about their practices.

Mexican witchcraft was exported from Europe to what is now Mexico, where it was combined with native practices. It often bears a sharp resemblance to other European-American folk practices.

To Mexicans, Spanish-speaking Americans, and some common, garden-variety traditional witches in the U.S., it is very ordinary to purchase a 7-day candle, some herbs or magical oils, and make a petition to the saints whenever there is a problem they need to solve or when they just have a need for a sense of peace and harmony in the household.

Despite this fact, in Mexico and throughout the Spanish-speaking world, witchcraft does not have a positive connotation, at all. The term, "witchcraft," as it is understood in the U.S. and Britain, is divided into two separate practices in Mexico: Brujeria and curanderismo, or witchcraft and healing respectively.

Brujeria is maleficent witchcraft mainly practiced by women but, also, some men. The practice encompasses almost everything that witches were accused of doing in the Middle Ages. Brujos (witches) are capable of laying powerful curses on people that can set off a series of unfortunate events in the victim's life. They use effigy magic, similar to western poppets and so-called voodoo dolls, which can be used to cause misery, insanity, illness and even death. They are very much feared by many Mexicans, including the Indians.

Curanderismo is the more benevolent aspect of Mexican witchcraft. Curanderos are similar to "root workers" in Euro-American folk magic and Hoodoo. They can break hexes and heal people. The magic of brujos can be undone by curanderos (healers), who are able to recognize the spiritual causes of some disease and perform healing rituals, like the Limpia (cleansing), and divination.

These Mexican healers know that some illnesses are caused by evil spirits or by spiritual injury. Children are especially vulnerable to the evil eye, so special care is taken to preserve their life energy from being taken, even inadvertently. This is why you may observe many Mexican children wearing a colorful bracelet as protection.

Curanderos are capable of seemingly miraculous, fast healing. They have techniques for breaking fevers and other illnesses, such as redirecting the unwholesome energy into an egg.

Like the U.S., Mexico is a very geographically large country. So, there are many remote towns and rural areas that are hours away from an allopathic doctor or hospital. Even now, many secondary highways between remote towns are riddled with potholes, which makes for uncomfortable travel even for perfectly healthy people. Therefore, it is still common among many Mexicans, especially those living in rural areas and very small towns, to have knowledgeable healers within the family or close community.

These are usually mothers and grandmothers whose knowledge is passed down to their daughters more often than their sons. They are knowledgeable in the use of plants, setting bones, and midwifery. Many Mexican children are born in the peace and safety of their own homes, rather than the prison-like setting of a hospital, a trend that is only just now catching on in the U.S.

Although there is less fear of the curanderos, both brujos and curanderos can do similar magic in the form of healing, casting spells, removing spells, and communicating with spirits.

In 1959, Hawaii became a state in the union, adding yet another fascinating dimension to American spiritual practices with its traditional religion. Unfortunately, their religious leaders have not been willing to share much of their beliefs with outsiders. Max Freedom Long is regarded as the major researcher and author on the subject of "Huna," which is Hawaiian spiritualism as it has been represented to the English-speaking world. Huna consists of a cosmological system that explains the structure of the universe, which is somewhat similar to that of Theosophy and not unlike some of the teachings of the Russian mystic Gurdjieff.

Since witchcraft has flourished, especially in out of the way places and among subcultures in the U.S., there is no reason to expect that it hasn't survived equally well off the beaten path in Europe and the British Isles.

Every nation worldwide, including those that have fallen under the control of the dominant religions of the Jews, Muslims, and Christians, still retain their old practices, even if they must secretly do so. This is true among many people in Africa, among the aboriginals of Australia, New Zealand, all of Polynesia, India, all throughout Asia and virtually everywhere in the world.

Even though the stories they use to explain the origins of the world and its history may differ, their practices of magic, healing, divination, conjuring, and spell casting are all remarkably similar, with fascinating and enlightening variations.

Up to this point, we have mentioned mostly lower magic or practical magic, but ceremonial magic has never gone anywhere, either. Although it was largely hidden from view until about the time of the Industrial Revolution in England.

At this time, there was an effort to increase public literacy. More books were published than ever before and even segments of the lower echelons of society began to take an interest in literature. Furthermore, there was a popular, nostalgic fascination with things of the Shakespearean era, including stories about ghosts, vampires and Faustian sorcerers who made pacts with the Devil. This served to revitalize popular interest in the magical practices preserved in old Western European grimoires from the 16th century.

During less literate times, similar practices of ritual magic were kept alive by the Rosicrucians, the Templars, and similar Freemason-style organizations. Not only did the practices not die, they were well-preserved within these orders.

The aim of old ceremonial magic practices from the grimoires is to control and communicate with entities, both light and dark, and to enhance the magician's own personal power. Because of this focus on personal power and sometimes necromancy and demonology, even now ceremonial magic is often associated with the Dark Arts.

Initiatory orders have long been a part of many old forms of witchcraft, particularly in times and places where literacy was low. This is especially true among the African-based systems, which were necessarily secretive and unable or legally forbidden to pass their knowledge on through writing. The safest and most efficient way of ensuring the survival of their knowledge from one generation to the next was to pass it on to younger members by word of mouth.

Formalized religion grew out of this necessity. Today, the leaders of these groups still employ a similar formal means of initiation and training in practices such as healing and divination. Although, just as with any established order, they are generally very dogmatic, often teaching members that their natural abilities are tied to the organization.

In past centuries, many people did not have a high level of literacy or have access to books on magical practices, so there was no alternative to joining an order or coven. Fortunately, this is not the case today.

Although it is true that not everything about witchcraft practices is made public in writing. Many things remain secret, although not necessarily because they are illegal or socially unacceptable, but because they are often highly personal.

## All of Us Witches

It is apparent that witchcraft is alive and well and always has been. This is because all people are inherently witches. We are born witches, which is why witchcraft cannot be eradicated.

The practice of witchcraft has never been dead, not for a split second. It has only appeared dead to a large segment of the population, the typical urban or suburban-dwellers who live in the dream world created by the male-dominated, heavily Judeo-Christianized mainstream media.

Such people are under the spell of the hypnotist in the living room, otherwise known as the television. It is the subtle dictator that tells you what words to say, what to buy, what to believe, and what is or isn't socially acceptable. It is largely the creator of an elaborate fiction. Many people are, also, directly under the spell of fear-mongering Christian preachers and their twisted view of reality.

People who have given their minds away to any authority figure tend to be self-centered and self-absorbed. Consequently, they are either oblivious to the natural world around them or hold it in disdain.

Television and movies are major tools of the mind controllers. Standing behind these elaborate fictional presentations are the men running the corporate and governmental institutions, who have the greatest interest in keeping people's eyes wide shut. They are committed to the status quo because it benefits their dominant position of power, the one they have maintained for a couple thousand years now.

It was their movies and their television programming that created the modern, popular conception of witchcraft. They don't portray the truth about witchcraft, at all. Instead, they present to the public a laughable, impotent form of it.

This has had a profound effect on the actual practice of some forms of witchcraft, in particular, Wicca. So, the modern mainstream of witchcraft practices, the ones that average people see and most newcomers are introduced to, are distorted and made to seem cartoonish. In this way, the mind controllers have done more to obfuscate genuine witchcraft than they have ever done to expose or rediscover it.

Because it is so largely predicated on fantasy and made to appear silly to most people, this false presentation of witchcraft in the popular media has been highly beneficial to witches on the whole. They have done serious occultists a great favor, although we have to wonder what their real motive is. Perhaps since they were unsuccessful in their efforts to destroy the practice of witchcraft, they opted to pervert and ridicule it, instead.

Despite these efforts, that which must now be called "traditional witchcraft" to differentiate it from Wicca and, moreover, what Wicca has become, has always been here. It encompasses many different practices by different people from different places. It has not remained static, but it has grown and evolved, merging with other forms of itself all the while. It has never gone away because it is natural and real.

The Spiritualist movement, which began in New York in the 1830s, grew out of this natural state of affairs. It is perfectly normal and natural for children to see spirits and for young girls to be acutely aware of the world of spirits around us. It was because of their inherent nature as witches that the Fox sisters heard ghostly rapping, which soon became a means of communication with spirits of the dead and led to a massive spiritual revolution.

The world over, seeing, hearing, and talking to spirits is a perfectly ordinary thing to do. It is equally commonplace to look for solutions to health problems in whatever you have available in your cupboard, in your garden, or nearby.

To those who make a study of worldwide witchcraft, it becomes evident that such practices are not only natural, but follow certain patterns, just as things in the ordinary physical world do. This observation of these hidden, universal aspects of nature is part of the study of occult science. It is a means by which to further understand and perfect your own practice of witchcraft. Such a student of the occult does not get caught up in quibbling over nationalized traditions or controversies about religion, because witchcraft supersedes all of these things.

## CHAPTER 9
## HOW TO BECOME A STUDENT OF THE OCCULT

Even among families in which witchcraft is an ordinary part of life, the family witch or healer typically spends a lot of time learning whatever he or she can from other sources, often becoming remarkably knowledgeable. Especially for healers, there is a hunger to know about the healing agents and techniques of healers in every country of the world.

It is important to have a passion for whatever aspect of witchcraft you choose to study and be a dogged researcher in pursuit of answers to the questions that naturally arise in your mind. Most serious occultists are passionate intellectuals with a broad knowledge of occultism along with a few special interest areas, in which they are experts. As researchers, they possess the obsessive curiosity of a detective. The more obscure and out of reach something seems, the more they want to get their hands on it. If they think a secret is buried somewhere, figuratively speaking, they pick up a shovel and start digging until they find it.

If you are not already an intellectual, you can easily become one in your pursuit of occult knowledge.

Choose a subject that you find interesting. It might be a particular order, like the Golden Dawn, or it might be a subject, like Spiritualism, astrology, palmistry, runes, tarot reading, or anything else that appeals to you.

Find the most authoritative books on the subject and begin there. Look for the origins and dig for the roots of everything, leaving no stone unturned. Look for the earliest related works and other important information. Read all you can on the subject, getting as much information and as many diverse perspectives as possible.

Take second hand information into account, but don't rely on it entirely. Historical accounts are often highly opinionated. Moreover, in the past, historians used different methods of constructing theories and providing evidence for them than they do now. Every writer, whether contemporary or historical, is influenced by his or her time, country, culture, and personal experiences and these things should be taken into consideration.

Be curious. Follow every lead. When you read the name of an author or other figure related to your subject, take the time to do a little independent research on that person.

If you have already have a background in one or more other languages, this is a great advantage. Any other languages you can read or speak will help you to increase your understanding and your ability to analyze what you read. If you are reading translations, look at the document in its original language to get a truer understanding of it. Translators often take undue liberties. Furthermore, many concepts either do not exist in the English language or simply do not translate well, so that important aspects of the original meaning are lost.

If you read a term you don't fully understand, look it up. There is no shame in not knowing the meaning of a word. Understanding the meaning of words and knowing their origins helps you make important connections between facts. Pay close attention to the etymology of words, which can be key to understanding their true meaning.

Don't just read books, study them. Keep paper and a pen by you. Make notes on the paper, not in the book. There is no point in reading a book without noting down important details, especially when you are making a study of any subject. If you find key information about something, make a note about where you found it, including page numbers, so you can easily find it, again. Even if you never refer to the note, again, the act of writing down a bit of information or putting a concept into your own words will help you retain it far more than if you just read it.

If you have a set of things, symbols for example, that you need to remember the meaning of before you can progress in your studies, obtain a stack of index cards and make your own flash cards. Draw the symbol on one side of an index card and its correspondences or meanings on the other. Test yourself until you know it by heart. This is learning by rote or memorization and it has long ago become unfashionable in education, but it is the only way to learn certain things, like the meaning of runes or the basics of the tarot.

When you first begin to move beyond the mere study of your subject and begin making practical use of what you've learned, start a Book of Shadows or a witchcraft journal for yourself. This is something like keeping your own recipe book. When you try something and it turns out well, write this procedure, spell or formula in your book along with any other pertinent information.

Take advantage of the vast wealth of resources now at your fingertips. Research used to be much more difficult. You used to have to find a university research library or scour old book stores. Sometimes you had to pay a premium price for a rare or out-of-print book. But, because of the Internet, you are now able to go online and easily find a lot of books in digital form that used to be nearly impossible to get access to. All you have to do is type the title and the name of the author into a search engine to find it. Gutenberg (www.gutenberg.org) and Sacred Texts (www.sacred-texts.com) are good sources of old occult books, which are now in the public domain.

Take the time to analyze what you read. Try to connect the dots. If you develop a theory about something, do a little more research and try to confirm your hunch. You don't have to be right every time. No one is grading you and no one is going to tell you that your idea is silly or wrong because you are both teacher and student. The important thing is that you are asking questions and searching for answers.

Much like genuine witchcraft, intellectual inquiry is a subversive act. It causes you to question societal norms and even the nature of reality itself. The established order wants you to be an obedient, unquestioning sheep. This is what keeps their system in place and allows them to control humanity.

The religions of the world are mind control programs. All of us have been subjected to them directly or indirectly. When you begin asking questions and doing independent research, you are breaking your programming and that is the first thing you must do on the path of enlightenment. Asking a question is like striking a match in the darkness.

As you progress in your studies and, above all, the application of certain practices, you will begin to understand why some things cannot be easily explained. Books can be written describing certain processes, such as the unfolding of psychic abilities or steps to help you achieve certain seemingly miraculous abilities in healing and conversely in harming. But until you begin to make a practice of these things yourself, you cannot truly know what they are.

Books can only instruct you. They can only provide you with information. You have to acquire knowledge through practical experience. Seeing is believing. Until you see something for yourself, it is only theoretical to you.

Furthermore, some things defy explanation in ordinary words. In esoteric parlance, words can be used both to obscure the meaning of something to the profane and to impart information about it beyond the capacity of common language to an initiate. In many cases, there is no common language for such things. This is why sometimes metaphors are used to convey meaning or new terms must be invented for the purpose of a discussion.

You will often have to read something, study it from all angles, and then ruminate on it for a while. Crowley is well-known for providing information and then telling the student to "meditate" on it, which simply means to think deeply about it. This is an important aspect of studying the occult and sometimes it is the only way to find the answers you're looking for.

# CHAPTER 10
## ON COMING OUT OF THE CLOSET

It is common, especially in Wiccan social circles, to talk about coming out of the closet as a witch. In some areas of the country, there are now large numbers of witches of all kinds, and many of them live openly and rarely, if ever, encounter any discrimination or harassment. The most open are Wiccans because they are the most socially acceptable and may even have the greatest numbers among occultists in the U.S, although this is debatable and there is no way to know for sure.

But most serious occultists are in the closet to some degree, especially those involved in less widely accepted practices. These include Satanism, Luciferianism, Santeria, Hoodoo, and traditional witchcraft. In other words, nearly all occultists except Wiccans are closeted.

Despite all of the talk about coming out of broom closets, there are real dangers involved in doing so, depending on your circumstances. You will likely have far fewer problems being out of the closet in a big city or in areas where there is a great deal of tolerance for occultists, such as Salem, Massachusetts, where they seem to really have an appreciation for witches.

In fact, if you live in one of these areas, you probably cannot imagine the problems that can come with being out of the closet in a place dominated by Christians. It's something that almost has to be seen to be believed.

If you live in a small town or rural area of the U.S., especially one surrounded by Evangelicals or other militant Christians, you may want to be careful about who you allow to see your personal library. In fact, it is not recommended that you come out of the closet in such instances unless you must, for example, because you make your living as a psychic, an astrologer, or the owner of a metaphysical bookstore.

You may encounter major hassles in such areas, although usually your persecutors are subtle. It isn't just that they are not nice, they can make your life miserable. For example, they may refuse to lease to you, or you may have difficulty getting delivery of your mail or other services. Of course, this may be illegal, but there's not really much you can do about it and the perpetrators know this, so it goes on.

Some types of Christians feel that it is their duty to try to convert you or, at least, rebuke you, which can lead to a very tense situation if you have to work with such a person. They may become very frightened, even around Wiccans, as harmless as they are, because they are convinced that they worship Satan and cast evil spells. Nothing the Wiccan or anyone else can say in their defense will dissuade them from this belief. Consequently, they may act out of both fear that some curse might be placed upon them and out of a sense of moral duty to save you from the certainty of eternal Hell.

Many Wiccans and other neo-pagans believe that if they approach their enemies with a positive and open attitude, they can simply reason with them, and they will surely see how harmless, loving, and good-intentioned they are and, at least, agree to disagree. Sometimes this is true, but it is not always so.

On more than one occasion, the author has witnessed first hand the terror of Christians who find they have entered the premises of a witch-owned business. They react like people possessed by demons, bending over at the waist, holding their stomachs like they're about to regurgitate newts and frogs, while shrieking about the existence of pentagrams and other "tools of the Devil." This may sound funny, but it is actually very sad to see people so full of fear that they become almost physically ill. This illustrates what they really think about witches, witchcraft, and anything to do with the occult. They are mortally terrified of it.

So, it may not be that they are simply harassing or trying to prevent you from exercising your natural and legal right to practice your religion or other beliefs just because they're jerks. It may be that they are truly afraid of you.

The truth is, even though Wicca has attained a degree of acceptance, you can have a lot of problems if the wrong people know you are a witch. You cannot rely on First Amendment protections in all instances, especially if you have children. If you ever endure a divorce and have a custody battle, your judge may not be sympathetic to witches.

While it is true that it is illegal to fire people on the basis of religion, this won't keep an employer from firing you for "other" reasons or mistreating you in some way. Witches who come out of the closet, also, run the risk of losing their relationships with friends and family members.

This is why you should make a careful analysis of your particular circumstances before you step out of any broom closets and openly announce your interest in the occult.

Keep this in mind when you are talking to people from other countries, especially in Latin America or the Caribbean. Witchcraft is a very serious matter in some other countries. If you tell them you are a witch, they are probably going to think you are either dangerous or insane. It's not going to make a very good impression on them. It is likely they have never considered witchcraft in terms of being a benign religious practice because this idea is contrary to all they know about the subject.

Many people have been taught to be honest at all costs. In reality, this usually only makes you a target. You have no obligation under the laws of nature to give people information that they might be able to use to harm you. Therefore, it is not necessary to tell everything you know.

In places where Wicca has a little more acceptance, many non-Wiccan witches, if asked, will say they are Wiccan. This is a white lie that hurts no one. You have no obligation to give an honest answer to an impertinent inquiry into your personal life, even if the person making the inquiry probably means no harm. The fact is, it's none of their business.

If you don't want to tell even a white lie, then just don't say anything. You never have to answer a question from anyone.

You are not a lesser person, a coward, or any other such thing if you choose to remain silent about your interests. Remember: Discretion is the better part of valor. Furthermore, it is perfectly normal to not enjoy being seen as a curiosity or recoiled from in horror.

Furthermore, many traditional witchcraft practices, especially those involving black magic or demonology, are not well received by other witches, especially by Wiccans and many other neo-pagans. Discussing it with them will only invite ridicule, cruelty, or some destructive action against you, even by some of those who claim to be tolerant of other people's chosen paths.

Consider whether it would make your life easier or harder if you were to allow others to know about your practices. Choose your confidants wisely. Ultimately, do whatever you think will be most beneficial to you in your particular situation.

Just be aware that many of our oppressors are genuinely fearful, which makes them both pathetic and potentially dangerous, exactly as they have always been all throughout history.

## CHAPTER 11
## WHAT'S NEXT AFTER WICCA?

You don't have to actually leave Wicca to begin studying other types of witchcraft or other things to do with the occult. Wicca is the safe place from which many people do this.

It is especially helpful if you're just not ready to give up the idea of having some kind of religion. Religion provides the comfort of believing we have the answers to life's most pressing questions and it gives us the sense that we won't fall into danger or do something immoral.

Wicca is not the most restrictive religion. But it does create some psychological obstacles for people and you should just be aware of these so you can acknowledge them and decide what, if anything, you want to do about them.

These obstacles to progress are as follows:

1.) Wicca leaves people with the impression that no witches did any of the things they were accused of by their neighbors and the witch hunters, including consulting with dark entities. Although it must surely seem strange to Wiccans who are taught to believe that witches never cavorted with devils or cast vengeful spells that there are so many of these accusations and artistic depictions of such things.

While many perfectly innocent people, especially those with property that could be forfeited to the state, were caught up in the witch craze, it is more than likely that there were still witches who did exactly the kinds of things they were accused of doing. We can very safely surmise this because such people and practices still exist. They never died out, and it is an absolutely undeniable fact that many of these western European practices were exported to The Americas where they survive to this day.

2.) Wiccans often completely dismiss the idea of evil on the basis that nature is neither good nor evil. Also, they tend to believe that most people are basically good and that especially all witches are good. These are beliefs that could get you into some trouble.

The truth is that not all witches are good. Bad witches do exist just as evil exists. Some fortunate people live their entire lives without coming face to face with true evil, but once you've seen it you can never be disillusioned.

There are some ugly things going on in this world, especially in some parts of the U.S and Mexico, where human life is considered cheap and crimes like kidnapping and human trafficking are prevalent. But the problem is not limited to just low-life gangsters or some individual psychopaths.

According to many different sources, crimes against children and hideous ritualistic abuse practices regularly take place, involving powerful political leaders and the churches, with the Roman Catholic Church commonly implicated. Prominent whistle blowers are such names as Arizona Wilder, Leo Zagami, and the recently deceased ex-CIA agent Ted Gunderson, just to name a few. Such evil is a worldwide problem that runs from the lowest to the highest levels of society.

So, you don't want to have the idea that evil does not exist, because it does; or that everybody who practices witchcraft is good, because they're not. Furthermore, they are probably not going to tell you up front what they do.

To illustrate this point, if you receive an invitation to meet a coven somewhere out in the desert, that you only know from online, you should definitely reconsider taking that trip. This has happened to some people and when they arrived at their destination, they discovered that the coven leader was engaging in human sacrifice.

Learn to be a little afraid of the things you should be afraid of. This will keep you safe. What you should never be afraid of is learning more about witchcraft and occultism, especially when your course of study involves reading books and doing personal research, rather than attending meetings in remote locations with people you don't really know.

3.) Wicca makes people fearful of cosmic repercussions to their actions. This fear can prevent people from experimenting with certain things or even reading about them.

Wiccan dogma, such as the Wiccan Rede and the Law of Returns, has absolutely no basis in either esoteric science or Eastern mysticism. It is balderdash! As such, you can safely ignore it without fear of consequences.

Here the saying, "The only thing we have to fear, is fear itself," holds true marvelously. Although it is a complete fallacy, if you allow the fear of "karmic justice" to take hold of your mind, you will only end up living in a state of perpetual guilt and anxiety, which accomplishes nothing except to make you miserable.

Who benefits from you keeping such ideas in your mind? Only people who want to rob you of your inherent powers and natural rights would tell you such a thing. Of course, many people are only mindlessly repeating what they have been told.

But this is a belief that restricts you and keeps you from fully exploring all aspects of nature. The word, "nature," is used here in the esoteric sense to mean both the seen and unseen aspects of the world and the occult science that is used to explain it all. By contrast, when Wiccans use the word, "nature," they often take it literally to mean the great outdoors.

Of course, this is not a license to run out and commit some violent crime or rob a liquor store. But chances are you weren't going to do something like that, anyway. So, you can dispense with these restrictive, Christian-like, Wiccan notions whenever you are ready. Not only will no harm come to you, but you will learn to trust yourself. You will learn the nature of your own will, and how to wield it.

After all, this is the purpose of witchcraft. This is why the most castrating aspects of Wicca are the beliefs in the Rede and the so-called karmic law, which did not even enter the canon until years after Wicca was founded.

## Where to Begin

If you have already begun an investigation of Wicca, you might as well make it a thorough one. Everybody is familiar with the latest books on the subject, and you probably are, too. But most people are not familiar with the more foundational books.

Take a good look at the essential works that support Wicca and the words of their founders. As you do so, remain open to any aspects of the occult you run across that inspire you to know more about them. Then find the best, most authoritative books on those subjects and study them. Some suggestions are given below by subject.

## Gardnerian and Early Wicca

Crowther, Patricia, "Lid Off the Cauldron," Muller, 1981.
Crowther, Patricia, "Witch Blood," House of Collectibles, 1977.
Crowther, Patricia, "The Witches Speak," Athol Publications, 1965.
Gardner, Gerald, "Witchcraft Today," Citadel Press, 1954.
Leland, Charles, "Aradia, or The Gospel of the Witches," 1899.
Murray, Margaret, "The God of the Witches," 1933.
Murray, Margaret, "The Witch Cult in Western Europe," 1921.
Valiente, Doreen. "Where Witchcraft Lives," 1962.

## Alexandrian Wicca

Crowther, Patricia, "One Witch's World," London: Robert Hale, 1998.
Farrar, Stewart, "What Witches Do," Phoenix Publishing, 1983.
Farrar, Stewart, "A Witches' Bible: The Complete Witches' Handbook," Phoenix Publishing, 1996.
Sanders, O. Alexander, "The Alex Sanders Lectures," New York: Magickal Childe Publishing, Inc., 1984.

## General Neo-Paganism

Adler, Margot, "Drawing Down the Moon: Witches, Druids, Goddess-Worshippers, and Other Pagans in America Today," Penguin, 1977.
Zell-Ravencroft, Oberon, "Creating Circles & Ceremonies: Rituals for All Seasons and Reasons," New Page Books, 2006.
Zell-Ravencroft, Oberon, "Green Egg Magazine," Church of All Worlds. (www.greeneggemagazine.com)

## The Druids

Nothing is really known about the Druids, but a number of books on the subject began to appear in the 19th century, mainly as part of an Irish nationalist movement. Therefore, the information in these books my be less than factual, but they are the basis for some Druidic orders and had an influence on Gardner and his early contemporaries.

Bonwick, James, "Irish Druids and Old Irish Religions," 1894. (www.sacred-texts.com)
MacCulloch, J.A., "The Religion of the Ancient Celts," 1911. (www.sacred-texts.com)

## Non-Wiccan or Traditional Witchcraft

Anderson, Cora, "Fifty Years in the Feri Tradition," Acorn Guild Press, 2005.
Anderson, Cora, "Kitchen Witch: A Memoir," Acorn Guild Press, 2010.
Fortune, Dion, "Psychic Self-Defense," 1971.
Huson, Paul, "Mastering Witchcraft: A Practical Guide for Witches, Warlocks & Covens," Perigee Trade, December 5, 1980. *Note: The movie "Season of the Witch" (alternate title, "Hungry Wives"), which borrow heavily from Huson's "Mastery of Witchcraft," illustrates the social context of the attraction of witchcraft for suburban women in the early 1970s.*
Cavendish, Richard, "The Black Arts: A Concise History of Witchcraft, Demonology, Astrology, and Other Mystical Practices Throughout the Ages," 1967.
Leek, Sybil, "The Complete Art of Witchcraft: Penetrating the Secrets of White Magic," Signet, 1973.
Randolph, Vance, "Ozark Magic and Folklore," Dover, 1964.

## Hoodoo, Voodoo, and Santeria

Gonzalez-Wippler, Migene, "Powers of the Orishas: Santeria and the Worship of Saints," Original Publications, 1992.
Hyatt, Henry Middleton, "Hoodoo, Conjuration, Witchcraft and Rootwork," Harry Middleton Hyatt, 1974.
Madsen, Claudia and William, "A Guide to Mexican Witchcraft," Minutiae Mexicana, 1989.
Yronwode, Catherine, "Hoodoo Herb and Root Magic: A Materia Magica of African-American Conjure," Lucky Mojo Curio Company, 2002.

## Germanic Occultism

Flowers, Stephen, "The Galdrabók: an Icelandic Grimoire," Samuel Weiser, 1989.
Kummer, Siegfried Adolf and Stephen Flowers, "Rune=Magic by Siegfried Adolf Kummer," Runa-Raven Press, 1993.
Thorsson, Edred, "Futhark: A Handbook of Rune Magic," Weiser, 2012.
Thorsson, Edred, "Runelore: A Handbook of Esoteric Runology," Weiser, 1987.
Von List, Guido, "The Secret of the Runes by Guido von List," Translated by Stephen Flowers, Inner Traditions, 1988.

## Satanism

LaVey, Anton, "The Satanic Bible," Avon, 1969
LaVey, Anton, "The Satanic Rituals," Avon, 1972.
Webb, Don, "Mysteries of the Temple of Set: Inner Teachings of the Left Hand Path," Runa-Raven Press, 2011.

## Luciferianism

Drowe, E.S. "Peacock Angel: Being Some Account of Votaries of a Secret Cult and their Sanctuaries," John Murray, London, 1941.
Howard, Michael, "The Book of Fallen Angels," Holmes Publishing, 2004.
Rahn, Otto, "Lucifer's Court: A Heretic's Journey in Search of the Light Bringers," Inner Traditions, 2008.
Waite, Arthur Edward, "Devil-Worship in France or the Question of Lucifer," George Redway, London, 1896.

## Gnosticism

Jackson, Nigel and Michael Howard, "The Pillars of Tubal Cain," Capall Bann, 2001.
Meyer, Marvin W. and James M. Robinson, "The Nag Hammadi Scriptures: The Revised and Updated Translation of Sacred Gnostic Texts Complete in One Volume," HarperOne, 2009.

## Theosophy

Blavatsky, Helena P., "Isis Unveiled," 1877.
Blavatsky, Helena P., "The Secret Doctrine," 1888.

## New Thought

Some good material came out of the early New Thought movement. But some of the later writers, in particular, seemed to be solely interested in making money with their books, often conducting expensive lectures and seminars. Their focus on positive thinking and prosperity, and misapplication of esoteric principles snowballed into what can only be described as massive fraud. This travesty does not, however, detract from the good work done by many early New Thought authors.

Atkinson, William Walker. "Thought Vibration or The Law of Attraction in the Thought World" The Library Shelf, Chicago, 1908.
Carnegie, Dale, "How to Win Friends and Influence People," 1936. *Note: While this is not an occult book, it is the foundation for the prosperity and self-help gurus of the neo-New Age movement. Perusing it will help you understand the roots of this movement and recognize their doctrines when you come across them.*

Coue, Emile and Richard Brooks, "The Practice of Autosuggestion by the Method of Emile Coue," Revised edition, Dodd, Mead and Company, New York, 1922. *Note: Emile Coue, a French doctor and hypnotist, was not a member of New Thought, but the above work, in which he writes the now-famous phrase, "Day by day, in every way, I'm getting better and better," was a foundation of later New Thought.*

Hopkins, Emma Curtis, "High Mysticism," Wise Woman Press, 2010. *Note: Emma Curtis was the founder of New Thought. She was influenced by the founder of Christian Science, Mary Baker Eddy.*

## The Golden Dawn and Ceremonial Magic

You have probably noticed that the word, "magic," is sometimes spelled with a "k." The custom of spelling of the word with a "k" at the end arose from the writings of Aleister Crowley who used this pseudo-archaic, alternate spelling to refer to his own form of Thelemic ceremonial or high magic. Presently, many people use the alternate spelling, "magick," to refer to other varieties of ceremonial magic, although traditional or folk magic writers still use the normal spelling. By contrast, many Wiccan authors use Crowley's spelling with the "k" to refer to all magical practices.

Bardon, Franz, "The Practice of Magical Evocation," Merkur Publishing, 2nd edition, 2001.

Bardon, Franz, "Initiation into Hermetics" Merkur Publishing, 2009.

Crowley, Aleister, "The Book of the Law (Technically called Liber AL vel Legis sub figura CCXX as delivered by XCIII = 418 to DCLXVI)," Samuel Weiser, York Beach, ME, 1997.

Crowley, Aleister, "Magick: Liber ABA, Book Four, Parts I-IV," Samuel Weiser, York Beach, ME , 1977.

Crowley, Aleister, "Moon Child," 1917. *Note: This is a work of fiction, but it features many members of the Golden Dawn who are thinly disguised as characters in the story. It gives the procedure for the creation of a Moon Child. There is some speculation that Crowley actually created such an offspring who is now the wife of a recent president of the U.S.*

Crowley, Aleister, "The Vision & the Voice: With Commentary and Other Papers (Equinox IV:II)," Samuel Weiser, York Beach, ME, 1988.

Fortune, Dion, "Esoteric Orders and Their Work," 1928.

Jennings, Hargrave, "The Rosicrucians Their Rites and Mysteries," 1870.

Kraig, Donald Michael, "Modern Magick: Eleven Lessons in the High Magickal Arts," Llewellyn Publications, 1988.

Levi, Eliphas, "Transcendental Magic," Translated by A.E. Waite, Weiser Books, 1968.

Pike, Albert, E. "Morals and Dogma," 1871. (www.gutenberg.org)

Regardie, Israel, "The Golden Dawn: The Original Account of the Teachings, Rites & Ceremonies of the Hermetic Order," Llewellyn, 6th Ed., 2002.

## Spiritualism and Spiritism

Crawford, W. J., "Reality of Psychic Phenomena, Raps, Levitation, Etc.,"John M. Watkins, London, 1916. (See Internet Archive: www.archive.org)

Hunt, Stoker, "Ouija: The Most Dangerous Game," William Morrow Paperbacks, 1992.

Kaelin, Angela, "How to Communicate with Spirits: Seances, Ouija Boards and Summoning," Winter Tempest Books, 2011.

Kardec, Allen, "The Book on Mediums," 1861.

## Old Grimoires

Modern ceremonial magic, necromancy, summoning, spellcraft, alchemy, herbal and mineral lore has some of its roots in many of these early grimoires. Many of the old grimoires below, along with many others, are available online at web sites like Twilit Grotto (www.esotericarchives.com) and the Hermetic Resource Site (www.hermetics.org).

Agrippa, Henry Cornelius, edited by L. W. de Laurence, "The Philosophy of Natural Magic," 1913.

Agrippa, Henry Corneilius, "Three Books of Occult Philosophy," first English edition, London, England, 1651.

Alibeck the Egyptian, "Grimoirum Verum," 1517.

Anonymous, "The Black Pullet: Science of Magical Talisman," Red Wheel/Weiser, 2007.

Anonymous, "The Secret Grimoire of Turiel: Being a System of Ceremonial Magic," Holmes Pub Group, 2005.

Barrett, Francis, "The Magus: A Complete System of Occult Philosophy," Red Wheel/Weiser, 2000.

Budge, E. Wallis, translator, "The Egyptian Book of the Dead," 1898.

Crowley, Aleister and S.L. MacGregor Mathers, editors, "The Goetia: The Lesser Key of Solomon the King: Lemegeton—Clavicula Salomonis Regis, Book 1," Red Wheel, 2011.

Dee, John, "Grimoirium Imperium." (May be from the early 17th century.)

Honorius of Thebes, "Grimoire of Honorius." (May be from the 18th to early 19th century, but purports to be older.)

Mathers, S.L. MacGregor, Translator, "The Book of the Sacred Magic of Abramelin the Mage," Dover Publications, 1975.

Mathers, S.L. MacGregor, "The Grimoire of Armadel," Weiser Books, 2001.

Mathers, S. Liddell MacGregor, "The Key of Solomon the King: Clavicula Salomonis," Weiser Books, 2000.

"Verus Jesuitarum Libellus, The True Petition of the Jesuits." (A nineteenth-century manuscript of conjurations.)

## Astrology

Goodman, Linda, "Linda Goodman's Love Signs," Harper Perennial, 1991.

Goodman, Linda, "Star Signs," Bantam, 1984.

Louis, Anthony, "Horary Astrology Plain & Simple: Fast & Accurate Answers to Real World Questions," Llewellyn, 2002.

Woolfolk, Joanna, "The Only Astrology Book You'll Ever Need," Scarborough House, 1990.

## Kabbalah

Crowley, Aleister, "777 and Other Qabalistic Writings of Aleister Crowley: Including Gematria & Sepher Sephiroth," Samuel Weiser, York Beach, ME , 1982.

Bardon, Franz, "The Key to the True Kabbalah," D. Ruggeberg, 3rd edition, 1986.

Fortune, Dion, "The Mystical Qabalah," 1935.

Mathers, S.L. MacGregor, "The Kabbalah Unveiled," 1912.

Regardie, Israel, "A Garden Of Pomegranates: A Outline of the Qabalah," Llewellyn Publishing, 3rd edition, 1974.

Westcott, W. Wynn, "The Sepher Yetzirah," Kessinger Publishing, 2010. *Note: The Sepher Yetzirah is an ancient Hebrew document concerning the creation of the world, expressed in esoteric scientific terms. A search for the words, "Sepher Yetzirah," online yields many different translations of it and commentary on the subject.*

## Gemstones and Minerals

Cunnningham, Scott, "Cunningham's Encyclopedia of Crystal, Gem & Metal Magic," 1988.

Melody, "Love is in the Earth: A Kaleidoscope of Crystals: The Reference Book Describing the Metaphysical Properties of the Mineral Kingdom," Earth Love Publishing House, 1995.

Melody, "Love Is in the Earth—Mineralogical Pictorial: Treasures of the Earth," Earth Love Publishing House, 1994.

## Herbs and Essential Oils

The subject of herbs and their uses is so broad that you will never find one complete book on the subject. The following are important herbals, including early ones and more modern ones with a focus on spellcraft.

Beyerl, Paul, "The Master Book of Herbalism," Phoenix Publishing, WA, 1984.

Culpeper, Nicholas, "Complete Herbal," 1653.

Cunningham, Scott, "The Complete Book of Incense, Oils and Brews," Llewellyn, 2002.

Cunningham, Scott, "Cunningham's Encyclopedia of Magical Herbs," Llewellyn, 1985.

Grieve, Mrs. M., "A Modern Herbal," 1931.

Huson, Paul, "Mastering Herbalism," Henry Holt & Co., 1974.

Hutchens, Alma R., "Indian Herbalogy of North America: The Definitive Guide to Native Medicinal Plants and Their Uses," Shambhala, 1991.

Kroeger, Hanna, "Heal Your Life with Home Remedies and Herbs," Hay House, 1988.

Worwood, Valerie Ann, "The Complete Book of Essential Oils and Aromatherapy: Over 600 Natural, Non-Toxic and Fragrant Recipes to Create Health, Beauty, a Safe Home Environment," New World Library, 1991.

## Spell Books

Buckland, Raymond, "Practical Candleburning Rituals," Llewellyn, 1970.

Buckland, Raymond, "Practical Color Magick," Llewellyn, 1983.

DiGregorio, Sophia, "Traditional Witches' Formulary and Potion-making Guide: Recipes for Magical Oils, Powders and Other Potions," Winter Tempest Books, 2011

Illes, Judika, "The Element Encyclopedia of 5000 Spells: The Ultimate Reference Book for the Magical Arts," 2004.

Kaelin, Angela, "Black Magic for Dark Times: Spells of Revenge and Protection," Winter Tempest Books, 2011. *Note: This is a unique spell book of practical magic especially for crime survivors and those dealing with official corruption. Part of the purpose of the book is to reawaken people to the idea that magic is a force for change in the real world.*

Kaelin, Angela, "Spells for Money and Wealth," Winter Tempest Books, 2011.

Kaelin, Angela, "Traditional Witches' Book of Love Spells," Winter Tempest Books, 2011.

Morrison, Sarah Lyddon, "The Modern Witch's Spellbook: A Guide to the Mysteries of the Occult, Explaining How to Cast Spells, Work Charms and Love-Magic, and Improve Daily Living Through Witchcraft" Citadel Press, 1971.

Morrison, Sarah Lyddon, "The Modern Witch's Spellbook, Book 2," Citadel Press, 2000.

Paulsen, Kathryn, "The Complete Book of Magic And Witchcraft: Revised Edition," Signet, 1970.

## The Tarot

You can achieve different levels of expertise in tarot card reading. The highest levels go far beyond the mere ability to lay out the cards and make up a story that makes sense to the person you are reading for. There are numerous manuals, which are all about the same, except they pertain to different modern decks. Regardless of your level of expertise with the tarot, the author's most recommended deck is "The Book of Thoth," by Aleister Crowley, illustrated by Lady Frieda Harris. Thoroughly study the little manual that comes with the book. It is very tiny, but it has enough information to begin reading.

Later, you may want to purchase Crowley's manual, listed below, to help you get a deeper understanding of his use of symbolism. But you cannot learn to read the tarot properly from any manual. You must study the Kabbalah, astrology, and the gematria in a systematic way and apply it to your readings. The following books are the most recommended. When it is done properly, reading the tarot for others is an important doorway to achieving advanced psychic abilities.

Crowley, Aleister, "The Book of Thoth: A Short Essay on the Tarot of the Egyptians (Equinox III:5)" Samuel Weiser, New York, 1951.

Kaelin, Angela, "How to Read the Tarot for Fun, Profit and Psychic Development," Winter Tempest Books, 2009. *Note: This book is a treatise that attempts to fill in the gaps left by most manuals, which reduce tarot reading to a mechanical process. It shows the process of developing psychic abilities through reading the tarot for others. It is not a tarot manual.*

Mathers, S.L. MacGregor, "The Tarot: A Short Treatise on Reading Cards," RedWheel/Weiser, 2008. (www.hermetics.org/pdf/Mathers.pdf)

## The Runes

Please, see the Germanic Occultism category above.

## Cheiromancy or Palmistry

Cheiromancy, better known as palmistry, is an esoteric science, more so than some other methods of divination. The study of palmistry is no light undertaking, but if you systematically study the work of the following two authors, then apply what you have learned to hands of every stranger you possibly can, you will eventually become adept and people will be amazed by your abilities. Learning this skill will, also, enhance your natural psychic abilities.

Cheiro, "Palmistry for All," G.P. Putnam's Sons, 1916. (www.gutenberg.org)
Saint-Germain, C. de, "Practice of Palmistry," Newcastle Publishing Company, 1973.

## Extra Sensory Perception (E.S.P.)

DiGregorio, Sophia, "How to Develop Advanced Psychic Abilities: Obtain Information about the Past, Present and Future Through Clairvoyance," Winter Tempest Books, 2012.
Dubin, Reese P., "Telecult Power: The Amazing New Way to Psychic and Occult Wonders," Parker Publishing, 1970.
Ostrander, Sheila and Lynn Schroeder, "Psychic Discoveries Behind the Iron Curtain," Abacus, 1977.
Yogananda, Paramahansa, "Autobiography of a Yogi," 1946. (www.gutenberg.org) *Note: This book is important because it shows you what is possible for human beings to do. It is an introduction to meditation, which is a prerequisite to the development of advanced psychic abilities.*

## Healing

Hardy, Mary, Dotty Newman and Marcy Foley, "The Alchemist's Handbook to Homeopathy," Delta K Trust, 1995.
Kaelin, Angela, "Magical Healing: How to Heal Yourself and Others," Winter Tempest Books, 2011.
Stein, Diane, "Essential Reiki: A Complete Guide to an Ancient Healing Art," Crossing Press, 1995.
Sui, Choa Kok, "Pranic Healing," Red Wheel Weiser, 1990.

## Occult Science and Technology

Occult science is the basis for occult technology and the foundation for understanding human abilities that otherwise seem impossible.

Adachi, Ken, "Orgone Adventures," January, 2004. http://educate-yourself.org/dc/orgoneadventuresindex.shtml
Besant, Annie and Charles W. Leadbeater, "Occult Chemistry: Clairvoyant Observations on the Chemical Elements," Theosophical Publishing House, London, 1919. (www.gutenberg.org)
Besant, Annie and Charles W. Leadbeater, "Thought Forms," Theosophical Publishing House, London, 1901. (www.gutenberg.org)
Copen, Bruce, "Healing by Bio-Magnetism: The Healing Power of Magnetism," 1960.
Copen, Bruce, "Prospecting via Radiesthesia."
Cosimano, Chuck, "Psionic Power," Llewellyn, 1989.
Dietrich, C., M.D., "Pendulum Diagnosis: Radiesthesia,"Translated by Bruce Copen, 1960. N*ote: For Copen's books and more on his methods and radionics devices, please see: www.CopenLabs.com.*
Drown, Ruth, "Theory and Technique of the Drown Radiotherapy: and Drown Radio-vision and Homo-vibra Ray Instruments and Their Uses," Society of Metaphysicians Ltd., 2003.
Powell, A.E., "The Astral Body and Other Phenomena," 1926.
Powell, A.E., "The Etheric Double," 1925.
Powell, A.E., "The Mental Body," The Theosophical Society, 1927.
Reichenbach, Karl, "The Od Force: Letters on a Newly Discovered Power in Nature and its Relation to Magnetism, Electricity, Heat and Light," Health Research, 1963.

## Final Words of Encouragement

Witchcraft was long ago driven underground, where it still remains. Although now it is covered by the slick veneer of Wicca. You will have to peel its decorative covering back, one piece at a time, to get to the real substance.

Witchcraft, as it is practiced worldwide, differs from Wicca in that it is not a religion and it does sometimes involve the acknowledgment of evil forces and dark entities. The truth is witchcraft doesn't make a very good religion, because it is essentially the opposite of religion, which exists to restrain people, take their natural power from them, and put their minds in a prison.

True witchcraft is not passive in nature; it is active and, at times, reactive. Magic—even black magic—may be used as a force for positive change in the real world.

Witchcraft is the essence of subversion, as such it is dangerous to any establishment that seeks to control others, which is probably why it has been diluted and made to seem ridiculous in the minds of the modern public.

If you have come in contact with the occult through Wicca, don't stop there. Investigate Wicca, then use it as a launching pad to catapult yourself to the stars.

As you learn more about the occult, don't hesitate to abandon a theory or idea when new information to the contrary comes along. This is all part of the process. The unsettling fact is that nobody has all the answers. It's something you have to find on your own.

This process of learning can be a little scary at times. Sometimes the information you run across will shake up your entire view of the world, but this is all part of the journey.

Reading about traditional witchcraft and occultism can only take you so far. Information can be shown to you, but real knowledge of witchcraft comes from a place within you. It must flow from your own experience. To obtain this knowledge, begin with the academic study of occultism and progress to its practical application. You must experiment with what you learn, just like a scientist in a laboratory.

In your search for the truth about witchcraft, you may find yourself naturally letting go of thoughts and beliefs that restrain your mind. As you proceed in the application of the things you learn in your study of the occult, you will experience things that defy your present world view. As you become more comfortable with these changes in your perceptions, you will begin to break away from all of those old restraints and finally fly free.

# REFERENCES

1. Coughlin, John J., "The Wiccan Rede: A Historical Journey–Part 3: Eight Words...," Waning Moon blog, February 2, 2002. http://www.waningmoon.com/ethics/rede3.shtml. Retrieved March 17, 2012.

2. Valiente, Doreen. "The Charge of the Goddess," Hexagon Hoopix, 2000.

3. "ACLU Defense of Religious Practice and Expression," ACLU website. http://www.aclu.org/aclu-defense-religious-practice-and-expression.

4. Zeena Schreck Discussing the Sethian Liberation Movement among other topics on U.S. radio show Nightwatch, YouTube.com, December 27, 2011. http://www.youtube.com/watch?v=a1Sm1QZ8KZQ. Retrieved March 20, 2012.

5. DeCamp, John W., The Franklin Cover-Up: Child Abuse, Satanism, and Murder in Nebraska," EducateYourself.org. http://educate-yourself.org/cn/franklincoverupexcerpt.shtml. Retrieved March 20, 2012.

6. O'Brien, Cathy and Mark Phillips, "Trance Formation of America," Reality Marketing, 1995.
www.trance-formation.com.

7. Valley, Paul E. and Michael Aquino, "From PSYOP to MindWar: The Psychology of Victory," Headquarters, 7th Psychologic Operations Group, United States Army Reserve, Presidio of San Francisco, CA, 1980. http://www.xeper.org/maquino/nm/MindWar.pdf. Retrieved March 20, 2012.

8. Joseph, Isya. "Devil Worship: The Sacred Books and Traditions of the Yezidiz," 1919. http://www.sacred-texts.com/asia/sby/index.htm.

9. Ibid.

# BECOME A PATRON OF SOPHIA DIGREGORIO USING BITCOIN AND ALTCOINS

For more details about our Bitcoin and altcoin patronage program, please, read the free ebook, *The Occult Files of Sophia diGregorio Bitcoin and Altcoins Patronage Program: How to Join Our Cryptocurrency-based Patronage Program and Why We are Doing Things This Way*, which is available at the following websites:

Traditional Witchcraft and Occultism Wordpress Blog:
www.traditionalwitchcraftandoccultism.wordpress.com

The Occult Files of Sophia diGregorio Wordpress Blog:
www.occultfilesofsophiadigregorio.wordpress.com

Psychic Powers and Magic Spells:
www.psychic-powers-and-magic-spells.weebly.com

Winter Tempest Books at Webs:
www.wintertempestbooks.webs.com

To join our cryptocurrency-based patronage program, please, contact one of our administrators:

**Max Goddard:** MaxGoddard@protonmail.com
**Kipp Kelsey:** KippKelsey@tutamail.com

# MORE WINTER TEMPEST BOOKS

If you enjoyed this book, you might enjoy other Winter Tempest Books:

*All Natural Dental Remedies: Herbs and Home Remedies to Heal Your Teeth & Naturally Restore Tooth Enamel* by Angela Kaelin

*Black Magic for Dark Times: Spells of Revenge and Protection* by Angela Kaelin

*The Devil's Grimoire: A System of Psychic Attack* by Moribus Mortlock

*Grimoire of Santa Muerte: Spells and Rituals of Most Holy Death, the Unofficial Saint of Mexico* (Santa Muerte Series) (Volume 1) by Sophia diGregorio

*Grimoire of Santa Muerte, Vol. 2: Altars, Meditations, Divination and Witchcraft Rituals for Devotees of Most Holy Death* (Santa Muerte Series) (Volume 2) by Sophia diGregorio

*How to Communicate with Spirits: Séances, Ouija Boards and Summoning* by Angela Kaelin

*How to Develop Advanced Psychic Abilities: Obtain Information about the Past, Present and Future Through Clairvoyance* by Sophia diGregorio

*How to Read the Tarot for Fun, Profit and Psychic Development for Beginners and Advanced Readers* by Angela Kaelin

*How to Write Your Own Spells for Any Purpose and Make Them Work* by Sophia diGregorio

*Magical Healing: How to Use Your Mind to Heal Yourself and Others* by Angela Kaelin

*Natural Remedies for Reversing Gray Hair: Nutrition and Herbs for Anti-aging and Optimum Health* by Thomas W. Xander

*Practical Black Magic: How to Hex and Curse Your Enemies* by Sophia diGregorio

*Spells for Money and Wealth* by Angela Kaelin

*The Traditional Witches' Book of Love Spells* by Angela Kaelin

*Traditional Witches' Formulary and Potion-making Guide: Recipes for Magical Oils, Powders and Other Potions* by Sophia diGregorio

*Traditional Witches' History of the Occult Banking System: How Witches and Occultists Can Use Bitcoin and Altcoins for Privacy and Anti-Discrimination* by Sophia diGregorio

*The Occult Files of Sophia diGregorio: The Public Monologues of 2018* by Sophia diGregorio

# ORDER OUR BOOKS WITH CRYPTOCURRENCY

To place an order for Winter Tempest Books using Bitcoin, Monero, Litecoin, Dogecoin, and other preferred altcoins, please, contact:

Kipp Kelsey: KippKelsey@tutamail.com

Max Goddard: MaxGoddard@protonmail.com

## SOPHIA DIGREGORIO'S CRYPTOCURRENCY DONATION CODES

Donate to the author:

Monero (XMR):
41wVxhAQchuESryqAQgnyhY7Qv4McnFrFZ6Sb
9ue16AdJzmGUMuBY6zP7cZ1JBG7nVfqJRUqW
zDBhayebZwae93pNkyFnMm

Bitcoin (BTC):
196qNENpoe8DGCt8mHYcm2xZ3oKZSxxyvq

Dogecoin (DOGE):
DBNNCYZe6WWPFZokjd933bm2eHLd9gAXzy

Litecoin (LTC):
La8aBs7BPVwP87tmKH9ggL1bVuoq2x866W

Dash (DASH):
XwTZaBxDSAxnAif3SWrkMUPhGSYXet5MpG

Bitcoin Cash (BCH):
14merNRUCMBHVJUDxb3q2ktdypUxiq4Qvu

Bitcoin Gold (BTG):
GRwsULUvqeHwCJ9V14J21b1GgS25KSz6S9

Zcash (ZEC):
t1f57jkSeiTLYMC1wcEWYu8BCLmRMDnfBmp

# DISCLAIMERS

The author and publisher of this book has used her best efforts in preparing this document. The author of this book makes no representation or warranties with respect to the accuracy, applicability, fitness or completeness of the contents of this document and disclaims any warranties expressed or implied. The author is not a licensed medical, legal, or financial professional, and is not qualified to give medical, legal, or financial, or investment advice, and nothing in this document should be construed as such advice. Any substances, instruments, procedures, or information described in this book should not be used a substitute for treatment or advice from state approved, licensed medical authorities, attorneys, or financial advisors. Any medical, legal, or financial questions should be addressed to the proper authorities on such matters. The information in this book is not medical, legal, financial, or investment advice and should not be relied upon for such purposes.

Nothing in this book should be construed as incitement to dangerous or illegal acts and the reader is advised to be aware of and to heed and obey all pertinent laws in his or her city, state, country or other jurisdiction. The statements in this book have not been evaluated by any legal, licensed, or government entity, nor any representative thereof. The statements contained herein represent the author's legally protected opinion, represent her best work, and are complete and accurate to the best of her knowledge.

The material in this book is presented for informational and entertainment purposes only and anyone who uses any of the information in the book does so at his or her own risk with the understanding that the author cannot be held responsible for the consequences. The author or publisher is not responsible for your use of or experiences with of any websites, companies, software, services, or products mentioned herein. The author or publisher shall in no event be held liable for any losses or damages, including but not limited to special, incidental, consequential or other damages incurred by, arising from, or related to your reliance upon or use of this information.

**FTC Disclaimer:** The author has no connection to nor was paid by any brand or product described in this document with the exception of any other books mentioned which were written by the author or published by Winter Tempest Books.

**Copyright:** What's Next After Wicca? *Non-Wiccan Occult Practices and Traditional Witchcraft* Copyright © 2019 Sophia diGregorio. All rights reserved.

**License statement:** This document contains material protected under copyright laws. Any unauthorized reprint, transmission or resale of this material without the express permission of the author is strictly prohibited. No part of this book may be used or reproduced in any manner whatsoever without written permission from the author except in the case of brief quotations embodied in critical articles and reviews.

www.ingramcontent.com/pod-product-compliance
Lightning Source LLC
Chambersburg PA
CBHW070628050426
42450CB00011B/3141